Self-Revealment

Self-Portrait

RAPHAEL SOYER

Self-Revealment

A MEMOIR

Maecenas Press   Random House

NEW YORK

TO THE MEMORY OF MY SISTER,

FANNIE SOYER MENDELSOHN,

AND TO THE MEMORY OF HER HUSBAND,

DR. ISAAC MENDELSOHN

Illustrations

Self-Revealment

October 25, 1967
====

My retrospective exhibition opened yesterday. In the morning I was invited to look at my paintings installed on the walls of the Whitney. I was tempted to go but was filled with trepidation. Instead I visited the Metropolitan Museum, to which I retreat whenever I need reassurance. There, absorbed in the paintings of the masters, my own work became less important and I felt ready to face my retrospective.

Just as I have always identified myself with New York City, so have I with its Metropolitan Museum of Art. I can say without any illusions of self-importance that the Museum and I have grown and developed together through all these years. I was taken there for the first time, a thirteen-year-old foreigner. For months afterwards there was a confusion, a montage in my head of fragments of Meissonniers, Gérômes, Pilotys, Makarts, Alma-Tademas. The dominating piece in this mental kaleidoscope was Rubens' dappled horse with its voluptuous tail. Then I began to go to the Museum by myself, or with my brothers, on Sundays, walking from the South Bronx across a bridge on the Harlem River. For a long time I was drawn to the rooms on the lower floor, then provincially filled with original-sized casts of Michelangelo's Medici Tombs, his Moses, some Greek Venuses, the Discus Thrower. With adolescent wonder I would look at the figures of "Day and Night" and "Dawn and Evening." These rooms were usually almost empty. Once in a while some lonely visitor would approvingly tap a cast and be alarmed by the resounding hollow echo.

I became interested in the American Wing, at that time consisting mainly of the Hearn Collection, with a portrait of Mr. Hearn himself, pink-cheeked and silver-bearded; a painting of a lovely mother reading fairy tales to her starry-eyed children; a woman in white among purple tulips; and many autumnal and spring landscapes.

Soon, however, I was aware of some other works in the Museum: a few Rembrandts, some Millets, a collection of small sculptures and drawings by Rodin.

A great day for the Museum and for me too, was when the Altman Collection was installed. By that time I understood, with some depth, Rembrandt's "Young Auctioneer" and his "Woman with a Pink," the Frans Hals', the Memlings and the portrait of a man with hands in prayer by Dirk Bouts, still a favorite of mine.

And then the Havemeyer Collection! with its wonderful profusion of paintings by Degas, the Impressionists, the El Grecos.

Paintings by Homer, Eakins, Sloan, Bellows began to appear on the walls of the Metropolitan. The Dreiser Collection of the precious Flemish pictures with the small, inimitable portraits by Van der Weyden, Hugo Van der Goes, was added. Brueghel's "Rest of the Harvesters," the Bache Collection and many others were put on permanent display.

I am acquainted with the Museum layout; I know its rooms, its walls and the particular location of the paintings I look at often. I studied in several schools for shorter or longer periods, but I did not learn much in any of them. My great school has been the Metropolitan Museum of Art.

April 2, 1966

My exhibition at the Forum Gallery is a sort of introduction to the forthcoming retrospective show at the Whitney Museum. There was a big crowd at the opening. In the sea of voices I heard phrases like "It's the event of the season." "He'll have a good press." I was excited to the point where I did not know who was there and whom I was greeting, a state of confusion heightened by the Scotch I was sipping throughout the afternoon.

I am always reluctant to have a show and I reacted against this one more vehemently than usual because of the scheduled retrospective; this would be unnecessary, I thought, and pre-climactic. Also, I was anxious to spare myself the artist's well known agony after his show has opened, the letdown, the feeling of uneasiness, of embarrassment brought about, no doubt, by self-exposure in his work.

And the critics, what would they say? While rationally an artist should be able to ignore their vagaries, the irrational fact remains that he is sensitive to criticism, is disturbed by it for a long period, making it hard for him to get back to work.

One may call this a theme exhibition. It consists of two major paintings: "Homage to Thomas Eakins" and "The Village East," and the studies from life for them. The "Homage" and how it came about are fully described in my book *Homage to Thomas Eakins, Etc.* "The Village East" is the result of my seven years' living and working on lower Second Avenue. I had become acquainted with some of the artists and writers, and I tried to capture the feeling of that area—the bearded, long-haired young men; the loose-haired, blue-jeaned girls with ecstatic faces; white mothers with Negro babies, against the background of drab walls bearing Fall-Out Shelter signs, above indecent and sentimental scribblings; barrages of green and red lights, and arrowed one-way street signs. I wanted to convey a feeling of energy and life in an atmosphere of deprivation and drabness. Like "Homage to Thomas Eakins," "Village East" is a painting composed of portraits, some of them well known, for example, Allen Ginsberg, Gregory Corso, Diane di Prima.

I have known Diane di Prima for many years. In the early 1950's she was a slovenly, fat girl with beautiful red hair who came to my studio with her female companion, a strong contrast to her—tall, small-breasted and full-hipped. They were obviously involved with each other, posed nude together, talked to each other about poetry, the theater, with an intimacy and mutual understanding that excluded me from the conversation. Once I overheard them discuss Ezra Pound, their great desire to visit him in prison, and their feeling of frustration in not having anyone to drive them there. I ventured to say, "He's a Fascist.

Why do you want to see him?" I still remember the lightning anger in their young eyes and their contemptuous retort that poetry had nothing to do with all that. Later I would meet Diane occasionally in the Village, without the other girl, but with some man or other, one of whom was the author Leroi Jones. Then one day she called to say she needed money and wanted to pose again. I painted her many times.

Now she is thin, her red hair in two long braids, and although still carelessly dressed, there is a greater display of femininity. She has three children, each one by a different father. She is full of an angry disregard for conventional living and behavior. I visited her in the house where she lived with her children and with Alan Marlowe, the father of the youngest one. It was an old, three-floor dilapidated house, with some broken windowpanes, rickety stairs, and holes in the splintery floors. Diane and Marlowe loved this house, it suited their needs for work and individual privacy. They made an attempt to decorate it with morbid sketches that had been used as stage designs for the experimental theatres Marlowe operated now and then in the neighborhood.

Diane is a sensitive poet, impatient with anything that is not avant-garde. She is an excellent translator of some very delicate poems from the Latin. I was repelled by her own volume of poems called *Dinners and Nightmares*, although I found them valid, real, and descriptive of a slummy, bedrugged intellectualism, in a terse, brittle, somewhat hysterical style. In my "Village East" Diane is the main character, aimlessly walking almost out of the painting, one hand in a pocket, the fingers of the other convulsively tensed. Her face is raised, her mouth partly open, her wide-open red-rimmed eyes are looking upward (Marlowe told me that she cries on gray days). ("Who is this girl in the red dress with the red hair and the red eyes?" someone once asked about her at a party.)

Like other avant-gardists, Diane is obsessed by Hinduism or Zen Buddhism and dreams of the day when she "will leave Marlowe and the children and go off to Benares, to meditate." She's of the opinion that our Western civilization is rotten and doomed, on the verge of catastrophe; she has no sympathy for it and no desire for it to survive. It was she who first brought Allen Ginsberg to my studio, who later came with Gregory Corso. She also tried to get Leroi

Studies of Diane di Prima

Jones to pose, but he was too busy and I had to use a photograph to paint his head in "Village East."

First Allen Ginsberg came up by himself, shabby, unshaven, but beardless, his black hair long and curly on his balding head, with a few strands clinging to his forehead. Under a dark blue jacket he wore a scarlet slipover on a blue denim shirt. He had the hollow-cheeked look of a young European-Jewish intellectual, and his lips seemed inordinately red in his pale face. As the painting progressed, however, his hair and beard grew, covering the hollowness of his cheeks, and his white teeth sparkled. He was beginning to look like a Hindu. He posed standing, patiently, and his warm, brown eyes behind the heavy horn-rimmed spectacles had a steady gaze.

Contrary to my expectation from rumors about him, Allen was unpretentious, sensible and pleasant. At the very first sitting we touched upon many subjects in our conversation. He found similarities between my background and that of his father. He mentioned his mother. "Do you know De Kooning's 'Woman'? That was my mother. Is it surprising that I am a homosexual?" He told me about a vision in which William Blake appeared to him. He recited some anonymous, precious, medieval poems with quiet simplicity. He talked about his recurring emotional breakdowns which sent him from one "nut-house" to another. He referred to his moments of ecstasy and wanted me to include in the painting a button on his lapel: "Legalize Pot."

Later, Allen brought to the studio his friend Gregory Corso, and I made a small painting of both of them. "I want to be in a picture with Allen," Corso said affectionately. Since meeting Ginsberg I have noticed that young poets and writers speak of him fondly, with respect, as if he were a teacher. I've learned that he's very helpful, gives a lot of time to them, and is liberal with his money. When he first came to pose I offered to pay him like other models. He asked, "How much do you pay?" When I told him, he said, "That's a lot of money. When I'll need it, I'll let you know." He never has.

8   At the time Allen posed for me I was still working on the large "Homage" which was always on the easel, with the individual portrait studies around it. He would look at them in passing, and once when I caught him at it I said I was

Village East

Artist's Sister

more satisfied with the small studies than with the large painting. To which he replied directly and simply, "But the big painting has an overall melancholy." When he happened to glance at the sketched-in composition of "Village East," he said, "Why don't you do something unusual and startling in this painting, like an erection on one of these fellows?"

One day he announced, "I won't be able to come for a while because William Burroughs is in town. He's my good friend and I want to spend all my time with him."

Gregory Corso posed twice for the small painting I call "Two Poets." I liked Gregory's face, at once saturnine and gentle, his shaggy tufts of hair, the changing expressions from moodiness to cheerfulness. This charming fellow, I was told, becomes obstreperous and belligerent when drunk. "I have to be careful not to get tight," Corso told me himself, "I'm liable to get into fights, and am often beaten up." The second time he appeared it must have been after a night out, or some weekend brawl. He was dishevelled, tired-looking, unshaven, and untidy, as if he had slept in his clothes.

On the Boat—June 22, 1966

This is the last full day of our sea voyage to Europe, and the boredom is approaching its peak. I think I'll start drinking earlier today, not wait till six o'clock. But first I'll do some dictating to my wife.

That's how I've been doing my writing recently: I talk and she writes down what I say. It is disjointed, planless and formless to begin with, but later on we try to put it into shape.

The *Oslofjord* is a small, pleasant trans-Atlantic ship. People are enjoying and praising the trip although the weather has been mostly cloudy. I am bored. I feel captive, enclosed, studio-less, forced into inactivity. I do not participate in the shipboard programs, except in eating and viewing dull travelogs. Little is

Two Poets

left but to look forward to the cocktail hour, which somewhat lifts my stupor, at least temporarily.

One pastime I indulge in is observing my fellow passengers. Besides eating, their main preoccupation seems to be showing off their wardrobe, men and women alike, and even children. There are many beautiful children on board and some excellent specimens of male and female youth.

A couple of passengers have caught my attention, one a "celebrity," an ex-diplomat, handsome, elderly, tall, without an ounce of extra weight, with an open, frank, absolutely non-conscience-stricken face. Blue, direct-gazing eyes, the wrinkles under them precisely drawn as if by the hand of a Van Eyck, with a serenity which Van Eyck's faces do not have. His manner is friendly and solicitous, as if it were incumbent upon him to be so.

Another fellow passenger is a college teacher, tall, round-faced, big-nosed and small mouthed, neatly and comfortably dressed, but with an easy carelessness. He is an introvert with a strong interest in people, soft-spoken, well-informed, considered in his opinions and with an eye for pretty women; the author of a forthcoming book dealing with some phase of human behavior. He too changed his clothes for the different occasions. I just changed my shirt every morning and wore the same suit all the time. I began to feel uncomfortable after a while. The last night of the voyage, for the final farewell dinner, I was prevailed upon by my wife to wear a dark suit and black tie.

I've been reading *Tropic of Cancer* on the boat. What would happen, I thought, if the Henry Miller of the thirties—hungry, unkempt and loud-mouthed—invaded this respectable assemblage? Or a guy like Allen Ginsberg, in slept-in clothes? What wouldn't Miller say about these people in his torrential eloquence! Or my sardonic friend Allen, what kind of a prose poem would he compose about the voyagers on the *Oslofjord*?

I am writing my third book. The first one was called a *Painter's Pilgrimage*, the second, *Homage to Thomas Eakins, Etc.* This one I think I shall call *Self-Revealment*, and it will be the last of the trilogy. Self-revealment! As if I have not been revealing myself since I first began painting. I'm still trying to understand why at this time, and at this age, in my sixties, I began this business of writing about myself, my work, my predilections in art. After all, my profession is painting and there, automatically, my personality is revealed. But here I am consciously talking about myself, "revealing" myself in this amateurish prose. Is this a preoccupation of old age, like reminiscing, or eating, or like touring? After all, as I remember myself in my adolescence and youth, I was the shyest, the most inward, non-communicative character, almost to the point of being retarded. In my early childhood I was told a story about an invisible hat. It appealed to me tremendously at that early age, and later too. To be invisible, unknown! . . .

How, and when, did I become eager to be recognized? As a painter I have attained some recognition in my country. Then to what purpose is this journal? I vaguely feel that, as I continue, this will become clear. Though I wonder.

If my father were alive today he would be one hundred years old, and my mother almost ninety. How brief life is! Suddenly I am no longer young.

My first memory—a young woman being pursued . . . trying to escape . . . the heavy calves of her legs . . . running around furniture . . . years later I asked my mother about this. Her answer was not reassuring . . . someone evil was trying to catch her.

Another memory, a more accurate one, of my mother struggling to make a fire in the stove, and the wood did not burn because it was damp, and she cried. There are other vague memories, of smells, smells of armpits, breasts, feet.

Recently, while reading Jones's biography of Freud, I came across two incidents in his childhood which also occurred in mine. The earlier incident: I wanted my mother to explain how we are made of earth, as the Bible says. She spat lightly on the palms of her hands, rubbed them together and showed me the particles of dirt that resulted. According to Jones, Freud related the very same experience and how impressed he was. So was I.

A later memory that Freud describes is not exactly the same as mine, but quite similar, and left a like impression. Little Freud and his, at that time to him, powerful father, were walking on the sidewalk, when they were ordered by a Junker—"*Jude*, get off the pavement!"—and Freud's father meekly obeyed, thus falling frighteningly low in the child's esteem.

My father came home one evening out of breath and upset. When my mother asked him what had happened, he told her, and I overheard, that two drunken peasants walking behind him said: "There goes a Jew, let's beat him up!" "What did you do?" asked my mother. "I made big strides." My all-powerful father sank in my estimation.

Speaking of Freud: My father was fond of telling what happened when my twin, Moses, and I were born. I was sickly, not expected to live, and had to be taken to a doctor some miles away. It was frankly hoped that I would not come back, since there was another child. I could consider this a rejection and an abandonment of me. Against all laws of Freudianism, I do not.

Another early memory: I had a toy, I don't remember what it was. I proudly showed it to a big boy. He said, "I'll make you a prettier toy." He broke off a twig from the tree we were under and cut it in half. He peeled the bark and with its lacy strips tied the two pieces of twig together, forming a cross. I still remember the moist whiteness of the twigs, the sweet smell of the peeled wood, the symmetry of the cross. I showed this beautiful "toy" to my mother. She looked at me seriously and said, "I'll make it look nicer." With a penknife she made some cuts in the wood, changed the position of the twigs, and the whole thing became tragically cockeyed in my eyes. I still remember my disappointment and how I held back my tears.

To try the patience of the mythical reader, one more early memory (and one that would delight an Isaac Bashevis Singer!): in the courtyard where we lived an infant died. A woman lifted the stiff little body and held it up for me to see. To my horror I saw a tail curled between his legs! I was frightened by this tiny *tchort*, *shedd*, devil. I never told this to anyone. I kept this in me. Many years later it dawned upon me that what I had seen was the dead baby's penis.

This was not my only fear. Lightning and thunder, terror of losing my mother, fear of God, and other religious and superstitious fears troubled my early childhood.

July 1, 1966

How friendly these northern countries are: Norway, Sweden, Denmark. How naturally colorful and unostentatious the people. The Norwegians are particularly beautiful in complexion, feature, and carriage, and they are tinged with an air of melancholy.

In Oslo I became aware of the stature of Edvard Munch. As it happened, there was an exhibition of Munch at the Guggenheim Museum in New York several months before I came to Oslo. Having seen some of his work in both places, I can now report how impossible it is to show pictures on the walls of the Guggenheim Museum, so broken up in space, so concave, so deadly white.

In the National Museum in Oslo and in the Munch Museum—these small European countries honor their artists by permanently displaying their life's work to excellent advantage—I saw a great number of Edvard Munch's paintings, drawings and graphics.

Like Daumier in France, Munch in Norway painted the collective face of his people. He did more. He captured the moody character and quality of his country's landscape, weirdly affected by the long days merging into white nights. This poetic morbidity of Munch made me think of the haunting loneliness in the work of Edward Hopper, my country's painter.

Daumier, Munch, Hopper: different eras, countries, even continents—yet in the Munch Museum I thought of these three artists simultaneously. The life-work of each passed through my mind. What fortunate figures in art they are. Like excellent machines with meshing gears, they appeared at the right time, their talents were sufficient, the circumstances were right, and they became the artistic exponents of their place and time. Unlike the Frenchman and the American, Munch was involved with sex and death, with fears, attractions, revulsions, an artist of the Freudian age. The titles reflect his themes: "Ashes," "Maiden and Death," the "Dance of Life," the "Cry," the "Dead Mother," the "Sick Child," "Jealousy," the "Day After." His scope was wider still. He painted children of all ages and sizes, singly or in groups, and old people. He was a fine and searching portrait painter, and his compositions of workers are unique in their social penetration. And his many self-portraits, from the earliest one with its proud Nordic features and abundant hair, to his troubled face enveloped in cigaret smoke, the tortured self in hell, his loneliness in a café, the insomniac wandering from room to room with the blueness of an opaque night in the windowpanes; and finally the frail old man between the clock and the bed. Looking at this, his last self-portrait, my wife thought of George Bernard Shaw who before dying said how tired he was of the limited world between his bed and the window.

Daumier, Munch, Hopper were separated in time by many decades. How timeless art is! When I see paintings that move me, I imagine my own pictures alongside of them and try to find my place. For instance, how would my "Homage to Thomas Eakins" look on the wall with Munch's paintings? Is my painting too rendered, too tangible? After all, I am working now, years after the element of abstraction in painting has become dominant. Munch's work does not seem to be out of kilter, it seems to fall naturally into this stream of contemporariness, figurative though it is. About my own work, I am uneasy.

In Munch's painting of the "Dead Mother" there is a child in the foreground clutching her head with both hands in shock and grief. I was familiar with this picture from reproductions before I saw the original. This child always made me think of my sister Fannie, who was a year and a half younger than Moses and myself, as she sat, her face cupped in her hands like an adult, while the house was filled with the moans of our mother in labor.

Fannie was the first to die (1963) of the brothers and sisters brought by our parents from Borisoglebsk to New York before World War I. This book is dedicated to her.

We were a dense pack of clamoring, greedy children. When our parents would take us visiting we were admonished by them not to grab from the table, to behave like guests. We would promise, of course, but grab, disregarding our embarrassed mother's angry glances.

As we grew older, our competitiveness became apparent. Sibling rivalry was actually encouraged in our house. Our mother and father were rivals, competing for our affection. "Whom do you love more?" a child would be asked, "Father or Mother?" If he would answer "Mother," Father would say, "Go away, I hate you." And Mother would do the same. Although a jest, it was disturbing to the child.

Moses, Isaac and I would show our drawings to our parents, and they would examine them for neatness and precision, then praise one above the others, thus encouraging rivalry. Isaac, much younger, already competed with us and very soon caught up. Except for our little sister, Rebbie, the youngest at that time, everyone in the family aspired to be something. Our father wrote his stories every morning; our mother constantly and bitterly complained about her lack of education, the lack of time for reading, for improving herself. Even in those early days Moses, Isaac and I were obsessed by childish dreams of becoming Rembrandts and Raphaels, whose work was as yet completely unknown to us but whose names we knew and revered. The atmosphere of our home was charged with overtones of ambition, frustration, rivalry and jealousy of one another's little triumphs. Once I secretly cried when my much younger brother, Isaac, made a better drawing than mine.

In this clamor Fannie was a quiet, proud aristocrat. Already then, she had an understanding and perception of human relations beyond the grasp of her brothers. She was steadfast, responsible, dedicated. Unlike her brothers, she loved going to school. I still cherish an early memory of Fannie in her padded, bright overcoat on her way to school, with Moses and me following closely behind, making mocking noises, imitating her gait, jeering, ridiculing her devotion to school, teachers, and marks. She was aware of what was going on behind her back, but ignoring our stupidity and cruelty, walked straight ahead without turning around. Once in a while, however, when her brothers' crudeness would become too much, she would say, "I have such bad brothers." We did not live up to her conception of what brothers should be. Her standards were high.

With time we became more civilized, even courteous to one another. But a shy reticence restrained us from showing feelings of affection. How deeply I now regret this lack of demonstrativeness. I should have told Fannie at least once how much I valued her. In my secret and intimate appraisal of her, I put her on a plane with a Marie Curie or a Käthe Kollwitz.

My mother married at seventeen or eighteen. There are still a few photographs that show her rustic beauty, pompadoured and high-corseted. These pictures are old, and their original rich sepia has faded, as has the photographer's name in ornate gilt letters. In later life my mother became heavy and dissatisfied with her lot. From my early childhood, as a matter of fact, I knew her to be unhappy. I remember the sad Russian songs she sang to me in a pleasant, simple voice, even when she was young:

> Why did my mother bear me
> And not give me any luck?
> It would have been better
> If I had drowned when I was little.

or

> My fate is bitter
> It is bitter to live in this world.
> How to explain the force
> That makes one cling to life?

When I asked my mother what these songs were all about, she would answer, "When you grow up, you will know and understand." This was the standard response to all my childhood questions by both my mother and father.

July 2, 1966

Can one attribute gender to a city? Oslo is strong, and yet neat, colorful, and femininely graceful. It abounds in statues of naked bodies of men, women and children. The vistas of Vigeland Park seethe with them, not only with statues but with bikini-clad bodies sunning themselves, and frolicking, naked children.

Like Bernini in Rome, the Norwegian Vigeland filled Oslo with his statues. Moralistically and repetitiously he dealt with human destiny through the medium of the nude of both sexes and all ages. Recently, the American sculptor Nathan Hale, with great personal effort, brought an exhibition of Vigeland's work to New York. It called forth no response whatsoever. I must admit that even I failed to see it. The name Vigeland had no meaning for me. But here, in Oslo, I am impressed.

His work is forceful, skillful, vivid and pictorial. He is concerned with birth, youth, fecundity, death, wisdom, innocence, love, struggle, friendship, sorrow and exhilaration. Vigeland Park is an unusual achievement in architectural planning and in sculpture, a combined effort of an artist and his city.

In my "museum without walls," to use Malraux's famous phrase, I have added to the collection of Rembrandts his "Oath of the Batavians." I don't know what the painting is about historically. In a semi-curve around a table, strange people of different sizes sit, stand and gesture. The main group is ceremonially crossing swords, in an oath of allegiance to a one-eyed, turbaned giant, the dominant figure in the composition. There is Rembrandt's universality about these inexplicable men. One of them, I could swear, posed for Rembrandt's "Isaac Blessing Jacob and Esau." The most fascinating part of the painting is in the lower right of the canvas: a carousing trio, painted in a fantastic, timeless manner, bringing to mind almost anybody—De La Tour, Fragonard, certainly Daumier and Goya—but surpassing and transcending them all.

Standing in front of this painting, badly displayed and lit in the old-fashioned Stockholm Museum, I said to myself, "Look at it long, study it. Who knows if you will ever see it again."

Sculpture by Vigeland
of Mothers and Children

July 3, 1966

To our great delight we saw in the museums of Copenhagen some unusual, intimate, unpretentious French paintings by Courbet, Corot, Daumier, the Impressionists, an unexpected Degas, some Matisses, including his legendary self-portrait showing the big, bearded head and slight shoulders, Gauguins and Bonnards.

Even apart from the museums, this first visit to Scandinavia was a happy experience. We walked the old streets of Oslo, Stockholm and Copenhagen and their waterfronts; became part of the crowds in the shopping streets that were for pedestrians only. My wife was absorbed in window-shopping. I was entranced by the pretty faces of girls, their dimpled knees revealed by their short-short skirts; and by the young, long-haired fellows. The human traffic was dense, colorful and exciting. I wished I had more eyes, in the back and in the sides of my head. Both my wife and I were especially enchanted by the beauty of the children. In each Scandinavian little boy we saw something of our grandsons, David and Joseph.

Berlin's Dahlem Museum—July 6, 1966

In the room of the Flemish masters, Van Eyck, Van der Weyden, Petrus Christus, and the Master of Flémalle, at the Dahlem Museum, I heard Rebecca say, "You know, Raphael, I understand now what you meant three years ago when you said you were not going to Germany but to the Museum in Dahlem, and to the Alte Pinakothek in Munich. Here I don't feel I'm in Germany; it could be anywhere in the world. Art is truly universal."

This gave me great pleasure, because it was hard to persuade her to come with me to Germany. Three years ago she refused to accompany me and I went by myself. Her comment referred to my response at that time when I was criticized for going to Germany. I said then, "It's not Germany I'm going to, but the Dahlem Museum and the Alte Pinakothek."

This time I was struck even more by the brashness and cheap glitter of *nouveau-riche* West Berlin. Culturally and esthetically, East Berlin again makes more sense, but even though it is more restored than it was three years ago, there is still a pall of sadness over it. Rebecca said, "There's something ghostly about these quiet, empty streets."

Now we are in Munich, absorbing the great art of the Alte and Neue Pinakothek. But every middle-aged German is suspect in our eyes. "What was his role in the Nazi period? Was he a stormtrooper, a member of the Hitler Youth? And these old people, how acquiescent were they?"

July 13, 1966

A short train ride from Munich into the town of Dachau, a taxi ride, and we found ourselves in the former concentration camp, the first of its kind, the training center for the S.S. men who were to run other camps. The gate led us through a double barbed-wire enclosure into the huge camp grounds. Where there had been thirty long wooden barracks we now saw thirty low, numbered, rectangular frames, fifteen on each side of a wide road, neatly filled with small stones. Still standing were the former infirmary and mortuary buildings, and one of the original wooden barracks, the windows of which were boarded up from within, their windowpanes broken. I wondered why these were broken when everything else was so tidy.

It was a beautiful day, and it was hard to visualize the hell that once reigned here. Nothing looked forbidding in this vast, sparklingly clean area in spite of the barbed-wire and the guard towers around it.

We went into the museum, an arrangement in black and white. White-washed walls. On black partitions, blow-ups of official documents, orders, edicts, questionnaires; letters from prisoners of one camp to those of another, a mother to her son, a husband to his wife; subservient, submissive and ingratiating letters from doctors to their superiors describing their diabolical experiments upon human beings; and blown-up photographs of other concentration camps and ghettos, some of them well known, of the Crystal Night, of a group of men, women and children who had just been rounded up, of a book-burning, of people lined up, faces against a wall, in the Warsaw ghetto. In this chronological and orderly arrangement of pictorial documentation, the most gruesome pictures were those under the heading of "Liberation," the famous photographs of the heap of naked dead, the mountains of shoes of those who had been tortured and murdered; and pictures of those who were dying from weakness and hunger while welcoming the liberation. One life-size blow-up of a little boy sitting on a curb made me realize the power of photography. No Goya, no Daumier, no Käthe Kollwitz, no Georg Grosz or Otto Dix ever created such an overwhelming image of the stark reality of a starving child.

I may add that in this museum building there was the usual museum desk selling literature and picture postcards to the visitors. There were excellent facilities for *Damen* and *Herren*.

Opposite the museum, at the far end of the camp, was a modernistic monument of a fluted, metal Christ on the Cross in a vaulted, stone structure. Beside it a *Versohnungs Kirche*, a Church of Repentance, was being erected.

We have seen other monuments and memorials on consecrated grounds dedicated to victims of Nazism, in Leningrad, Rome, Paris, Jerusalem, Rotterdam, and Amsterdam. How many more such places are there on the face of our earth? In Hiroshima and Nagasaki too, there surely must be neat and decorous shrines to those whom the American atomic bombs pulverized and mutilated. And after Vietnam—another monument? Another church of expiation?

We're in Munich now, but on this day in 1935—more than three decades ago, can it be?—we were part of the majestic outpouring of people in the streets of Paris in the famous Front Populair demonstration. It was Bastille Day. Tall, thin, Henri Barbusse was at the head of the procession, followed by old soldiers, survivors of the Paris Commune, their chests covered with medals and ribbons, by veterans of the First World War, many of them on crutches and in wheelchairs, and then—a surging sea of humanity. Especially vivid in my memory is the multitude of Algerians, arms interlocked, and all the others, young and old, filling the wide street from curb to curb, shouting *"A bas la guerre! A bas la guerre!"* The sidewalks and every window were crowded with spectators, pouring confetti, joining in the slogans, waving flags or holding out pillows in red ticking. The very houses seemed animated. We followed the route of march . . . was it from the Place de la Bastille to La République, or from Nation? I don't know any more, but it terminated at the Place de La République, and it seemed to us in our state of exultation that this huge maternal La République opened her ample arms to welcome her united people.

We were young then, married a few years, and this demonstration gave us hope for the future. In spite of the nightmare that followed, we shall never forget that day.

In West Berlin we saw an inadequate exhibition called *"Von Neue-Sachlichkeit zu Kein-Sachlichkeit,"* that is, "from new objectivism to non-objectivism." The most important exponent of Neue-Sachlichkeit, Otto Dix, was not even represented, but I did have the great satisfaction of seeing one of those extraordinary early paintings by Georg Grosz: a cross-eyed, cruel, duel-scarred Junker in the foreground; a blind ex-soldier tapping the sidewalk with his cane, and a Dostoevskian dog. A meager painting in color and metier, more a drawing in gray and black. *"Und doch!"* as the Germans say.

Artist's Father

In front of paintings by Georg Grosz I become so dissatisfied with the mildness, the "sympathy," the unexaggeratedness of my art.

In a civic gallery in Berlin we saw an exhibition called "75 Years of German Graphic Art." For some reason, Georg Grosz was not represented, but Käthe Kollwitz and Max Beckmann were. I was most impressed by a small etching, by Otto Dix, of an episode of World War I—a low-flying airplane strafing a city street. In the foreground, people run frantically, mothers clutching children. It could be Guernica, or any other bombed place. I imagined this 6×8 etching blown up to the proportions of Picasso's "Guernica." Perhaps it would lack the cherished esthetics of that mural, but how much more authentic, more moving and more shocking it would be.

July 18, 1966

In a sense my father was lucky not to know that Hitler's program of genocide would destroy six million Jews. But he also did not live to see the establishment of the State of Israel. He was an enthusiastic Zionist all his life, yet never had a chance to visit Palestine because he was unable to save enough for the trip. That many of his colleagues and contemporaries did manage to do so made him more keenly disappointed, even resentful. Towards the end of his life things became easier, the children were grown, and both he and my mother began to hope to settle in Palestine. Then it was too late. Illnesses began to plague them.

When we were very young our father would drag the older children, Moses, Fannie, myself, and maybe Isaac to Zionist meetings where emotional, nationalistic oratory was always followed by the singing of *Hatikvah*. Usually we were the only children present, and I still have a clear picture of my father, out of whose full-lipped, open mouth, framed by a black, round beard, poured resonantly forth:

> Our hope is not yet lost . . .
> To return to the land of our fathers.

He had the glazed look of one who saw glories of realized dreams.

Russian and Hebrew were the two languages in our home. Russian for obvious reasons: it was the language of our environment and school. Hebrew we learned by osmosis. Our father was the Hebrew scholar and teacher of Borisoglebsk. He had no time to teach us directly. But (again to use the word *drag*) he would drag us to the homes of his private pupils where, while ostensibly teaching them, he hoped that we would benefit by that instruction. And we did.

Artist's Father

Artist's Mother

I'm still amazed every once in a while at how much of the Hebrew language, which I absorbed then, I still retain.

My father was also a Hebrew writer. He wrote children's tales, and for adults short stories and novelettes in the style of Chekhov. His children's book *From the World of Wonders,* and the two volumes of *The Passing Generation* and other titles may still be found in some stockrooms of bookstores and libraries here and in Israel. He would write early in the morning, a habit formed in Russia which continued the rest of his life. He would cut wrapping paper into long strips, which he covered with very straight lines of his beautiful Hebrew script. I often wondered why he used wrapping paper. Probably because we were poor and writing paper was costly and scarce. For many years there were rolls and rolls of them in our house. What finally became of them, I don't know.

It may have been shortly after our father's death that we found a bundle of old love letters from him to our mother. Her name was Bella, and in those letters he called her Belka, or Belotchka, which means both "little squirrel" and "little white one" in Russian. To translate freely as much as I remember, my father wrote: "My dear Belka, I will caress you, I will indulge you and spoil you, I will provide for you. You will never have to exert yourself," and other endearing promises. But after they were married these promises were apparently unfulfillable. A dark legend persisted in our family that promptly after marriage our father lost our mother's dowry in a lumber venture in some Lithuanian forest and became a *knecht* (Yiddish for "slave") to a lumber tycoon by the name of Avrom Kavnat. I knew this sinister name all through my childhood.

Perhaps my mother's melancholy spirit owed its origin to the early dis-illusionment caused by this unfortunate crisis. She acquired a propensity for silent weeping, which would come upon her suddenly, often for no apparent reason. This persisted throughout her life, and finally developed into the illness from which she never recovered. Yet she had a sense of humor, was earthy, and functioned normally, I should say remarkably, raising her brood of children. It was my mother who taught me to write the Russian alphabet in shaded monogram letters. In school I was noted for my excellent penmanship.

Now that I can look back upon all this with some comprehension, I can

25

see that my father was not meant to be a businessman. He was a naïve poet, a romantic, a hero-worshipper; he loved pictures, statues, monuments. He decorated the cold and dreary walls of our home in Borisoglebsk with postcard reproductions of Russian paintings, in fan-shaped designs. It was from our father that we first heard the names of Rembrandt, Raphael, Michelangelo. He could draw, too. He would make pictures of Cossacks on horses and all the trimmings on both of them, the horses in prancing position showing their horseshoes, the Cossacks brandishing their sabres. Moses and I would copy these pictures, and I still remember how hard it was to draw horseshoes on hoofs. My father would "correct" these drawings and exhibit them as our own to friends, and to the young "gymnasists" and students who were constant visitors in our home. These young fellows in their brass-buttoned uniforms and visored caps were helped by our father in their compositions, and they in turn would devotedly coach us in arithmetic, spelling, and other subjects, much to our annoyance.

Our father also drew designs for tablecloths and other linens which our mother embroidered skillfully and colorfully. Some of them were complicated, of troikas, or of soldiers saying goodbye to their wives, and were copied from illustrations in poetry books. But he also made his own designs of leaves, flowers, berries and chirping birds. The color schemes were always our mother's.

One evening, a young man named Ivan Ivanovich Pozdniakov, came to our house and did a drawing of our father from life. That one could draw a living person was a sudden revelation to me. I stopped drawing for several days, then asked my father to pose for me as he had for Ivan Ivanovich. When the drawing was praised, my elation was boundless. From then on I became a confirmed realist. I drew only from nature rather than from imagination, like other children. In retrospect, I believe that this limited my art, but perhaps my love for painting people stems from that incident.

As time went on I made more discoveries. There was a wood in the outskirts of town to which our father would take us on Sundays, to picnic and to draw. Even in those days, I was fascinated in a childish way by space and perspective. But I was always frustrated by my inability to indicate on paper the difference between the trees close to me and those far from me. One day I saw a picture of a forest in a magazine and I noticed that the nearer trees began at the bottom of the paper and as the trees receded, the farther up the paper they were. How this illusion of distance from tree to tree was effected was another revelation. I made many drawings of our woods according to this guideline, and I never ceased to wonder at the space and distance I was able to create on the flat surface of the paper.

Again, I discovered that by shading one can give a third dimension of roundness and solidity, and once while making a picture of the ever-present rubber plant, I added some green to the leaves and was startled by the additional touch of reality this gave to my drawing. I was acquiring the habit of drawing the visible world, and with it the discipline that comes from daily application.

Vienna—July 20, 1966

I am always swept off my feet by the variety and profusion of the paintings in Vienna's Kunsthistorisches Museum. I looked again so long and intently at the three self-portraits of Rembrandt, the inimitable and artistically infallible children by Velásquez, Vermeer's studio, the Brueghels and Titians, the Holbein portraits, the Dürers and Van Eyck's "Albergati," that I feared the black spots always floating in my vision would turn into flashes of light again. (This had happened once when my eyes were over-strained, and I worriedly consulted a doctor.)

The Viennese seem to love statues almost as much as pastries. In a park we read an announcement saying that on this spot a monument will be erected to someone. As if Vienna lacks monuments or statues. They're all over the place: in public squares, in the middle of streets, in parks among trees and bushes can be seen statues of equestrians, of men and women in marble and bronze, sitting, standing, reclining, gesturing, all on lavish pedestals. On housetops they stand dangerously close to the edge, as if ready to jump. Even riders on prancing horses and chariots are up there overhead. Not to mention the fountains with their naked nymphs and cherubs, and the numerous churches with all the holy statuary inside and out.

We saw mostly older people in Vienna. They sat decorously on park benches, or in the outdoor cafés, genteelly consuming ice cream and pastry, or strolled sedately on the clean streets. We missed the young people who so animated the streets of Oslo, Stockholm, Copenhagen.

Vienna's Museum of the Twentieth Century was a disappointment, both in its supermarket-like exterior and in its meager contents. There were a few good pictures—a couple of Klimts, an Egon Schiele of characteristic intensity, an early Kokoschka portrait, early Jawlenskys, a few Kirchners and Schmidt-Rottluffs, a Guttuso. None of them masterpieces. The rest was the usual sort of thing that by now we are accustomed to, and expect to see in a "Twentieth Century" museum.

Twentieth century museum! In another thirty years or so, if this pattern of fashion in art of a *dernier cri* persists, then, to continue this ephemerality, a twenty-first century supermarket for art will have to be built. And if, as in everything else, this trend is accelerated, then perhaps every decade a new pre-fab will be assembled to contain the art of that moment.

The Guttuso was a simple picture of a young woman with two convulsive hands, one clutching a white cloth against her groin, the other on her chest, her wild-eyed head thrown back. Except for this cloth and the position of the head, the painting recalled the traditional Medici-Venus pose.

Standing before this painting I was again assailed, as I often am, by doubts about my own work. It is painted so uninhibitedly, so freely, with deliberate avoidance of the refinement one gets from many repaintings; and hastily, preserving the artist's immediate reaction. I voiced my misgivings to my wife. She said, "But you go deeper than this. You get more psychological insight. You probe deeper." Then I called her attention to the colors in the picture, the yellow ochre tinged with the gray of the flesh tones. "He, too, probes deeply," I said. "He expresses not only the living body, but hints also at its inherent deterioration. When I paint a nude, I'm also interested in the 'livingness' of it, and I too try to express what time will do to it. But in my desire to get a quality that can be attained only by many repaintings, I lose sight of this aim which Guttuso is able to realize by painting quickly. And then the Guttuso painting does have a quality all its own which, I suppose, is twentieth-century expressionism. I envy this ability to paint hastily, with momentary enthusiasm, without refinements, finesse, or regard for accuracy, precision, proportion. Compared to Guttuso and others, I feel out of my time. Accuracy, proportion, even likeness, concern me when I paint."

Rome—July 22, 1966

Although we enjoyed the museums in Berlin, Munich and Vienna, where I spent most of the time in contemplation of countless masterpieces, Rebecca and I felt relieved to be in Rome. Not even the treasures of Dahlem, of the Pinakothek, and of the Kunsthistoriches Museum could erase from our consciousness the barbarism perpetrated by the Germans in the twentieth century.

What is happening to Rome? Space is destroyed by automobiles, the air is polluted by cheap petrol, clouds of it spurting out from exhaust pipes. Throats are irritated, breathing is stifled. It's hard to get around in the heavy, noisy, honking traffic, almost impossible to cross streets. If this goes on, people will have to wear gas masks! How nightmarish! Imagine the people of Rome walking around with their handsome, expressive faces covered by gas masks. But I must admit that the young people, tourists and natives alike, seemed unaffected by all this; they are as exuberant and good-natured as ever.

Several months ago I saw an exhibition of Gregory Gillespie's work at the Forum Gallery in New York which aroused my interest because it was so unusual in content and technique.

Gillespie's studio at the American Academy in Rome was in indescribable disorder when Rebecca and I visited him. He told us he hadn't swept the floor

Gregory Gillespie

in two years because he didn't want his highly varnished pictures to catch the dust raised by sweeping.

"My pictures are offensive to some people," he said, probably because my wife was present. Reassured, he showed us his work.

Most of Gillespie's finished pictures were small and dealt with sex—more precisely, with sexual sadism: a fierce woman's head above naked shoulders and brightly nippled breasts, sinking gleaming teeth into an erect penis which alone, without the rest of the body, constitutes the lower corner of the composition; other small pictures of female figures vividly exposing their sex; a breach baby visible in an open vagina. There were two anti-war pictures—the face of a young man streaked with blood; a decomposed head in bas-relief, sealed in a shallow, glass-covered box, above which was a sign, "Fuck War."

30   What is unnoticed by others captures Gillespie's attention and preys upon his mind: a window in Naples; indecent drawings on mouldy walls; innocuous and ordinary photographs of fashion models, of ads for bathing suits, for

cameras or dog food. Extracted from their context, enlarged upon, these items become sucked into his work. The result is like distorted dreams, hallucinatingly concrete.

His technique combines many media, is involved and complicated. He cuts out photographs, mounts them and repaints them. A bathing suit ad becomes indecent, the water disarranging the suit to expose the private parts. He uses epoxy, glues, plexiglass, cement and seals his little pictures under layers of smoked glass.

I said, "Gregory, do you call yourself a painter?"

He answered, "Yes, a painter, absolutely."

I pointed to the head in the glass-sealed box and said, "You could have painted this directly on canvas. It would have been very effective."

There was something religious about these paintings—artifacts, I should call them, rather than paintings. Highly varnished, murky and tallowy, sealed in old cast-off frames under multiple layers of glass, they suggest icons and blood-streaked relics, with the guilt inherent in them. There is the same focus on punishment of genitalia as in the medieval depictions of sinners in last judgments.

Rome—July 26, 1966

It is our last evening in Rome. We had an early dinner in our favorite Piazza Navona, the one piazza which the Italians have not yet completely relinquished to the tourists. As if they said to themselves, "This is our piazza, not like the Spanish Steps, not like Via Veneto, not even the Piazza del Popolo. This is ours, with its three Bernini fountains." Here the people of the neighborhood gather, whole families, in late afternoon and evening. Children play here, jump rope, run, fall, ride tricycles. Women nurse their babies. Old men meet their cronies and young people stroll intimately, not like the promenaders of Via Veneto to look and be looked at.

Here, as I sit in the early twilight, I remember my youth: the piers of New York along the East River where, shortly after World War I, I wandered with my sketchbook on summer evenings, non-communicative and shy. Often I'd find a spot from which, unobserved, I would make drawings of people sitting around, talking, gesturing, eating, drinking, and of naked boys diving off the docks.

What a journey it was from Borisoglebsk to New York, by land and sea! A labyrinthian maze of third-class train interiors, of steerage corridors in old ships, of crowded halls in immigrant shelters. Our father, still in his prime, became known as the man with the big family. With his knowledge of Russian, Yiddish and Hebrew, with his strong voice and clear enunciation, and responsiveness to others, he became a spokesman for the immigrants. Many of their faces are still vivid in my memory. They crowded, pushed, quarreled, insulted one another, and begged forgiveness; they laughed, cried, and immediately worried about their reddened eyes. They worried about lice in their hair, for infected eyes and hair lice were the two main reasons for not admitting immigrants to the United States.

We were seasick. We ate bad food. There was some sort of sweet jelly or jam that Moses and I liked. We ate so much of it that long afterward we were able to belch it up and spit quantities of it out at will. Our baby brother, Israel, whose vocabulary had consisted of *pusti* ("let go," in Russian), which he cried whenever we tried to hug him, now learned another expression, *nisht gut* (Yiddish for "not good"), used all around him to describe the feeling of nausea, thus becoming bilingual very early in life.

I've been feeling detached from painting and drawing during this trip and, unlike other times, I draw very little. The pictures I have painted and those I've been planning all seem to be fading away. Except for going to museums, I spend my time thinking about and writing this chronicle. Again, what's the reason for this? What is there for me to report? After all, my life has been very uneventful, for I escaped wars, being either too young or too old. How I "free associate" in Piazza Navona!

Mention of war reminds me of a friend, a history professor who teaches at a college which he calls a "cesspool," a "prestige mill," and who has bitter and fantastic memories of war.

"Why don't you write your memoirs, now that you are planning to leave the 'cesspool,' as you call it?" I asked him once. His lips curled in horror, his eyes became sharp and abstracted at the same time.

"You know," he said, "if I do, I shall call it my 'Me-moi-res,'" combining the Hebrew word *moireh*, meaning "fear," with *memoirs*, a play on words. "Frightful Memories," or "Memoirs of Fear." What a title for a twentieth-century autobiography!

But I have no such memories. I escaped the apocalypse of Nazism too, safe in the country *Gdie niet Iudea i Iellena,* "where there's no Jew or Greek." This was how sophisticated Russian Jews described the United States when I was a child coming to this country.

I'm wandering off again. It seems I don't want to come to grips with why I am writing all this. Is there something in me of my father who filled rolls and rolls of brown wrapping paper with his constant writing? Lately, when I look at myself in the mirror, I seem to see him. All I need is his mustache and trim goatee.

How superficial is all this verbiage. I could dig much deeper if I had courage.

We had misgivings about Florence because we were warned that it was noisier than ever, that it stinks with gasoline; in a word, it was impossible. To our very pleasant surprise, we found the traffic more controlled, and the Piazza Signoria completely closed to cars. In the first book of this trilogy, *A Painter's Pilgrimage*, I referred to Florence as a "golden city." It is. The whole city is a work of art, a planned work of art, although it may not have been planned, so far as I know.

In the Santa Maria Del Carmine are Masaccio's murals. They are not over-whelming like the murals of Michelangelo and Raphael in Rome, or Piero della Francesca's in Arezzo. It is difficult for me to comprehend the imagination.

33

Mother and Child after Masaccio

fantasy, and skill of those three giants, but Masaccio I understand more readily. He is more my speed, so to speak; not turbulent, nor olympically serene, nor mysterious. His murals are not gigantic in scale, and their eloquence is without oratory, if one may apply such a phrase to paintings.

The "Tribute Money," is of a group of people, a horizontal composition all on one level in even height. What can it be compared to? To the "Brera Madonna" of Piero della Francesca? To the "Surrender of Breda" by Velásquez? Or to Courbet's "Burial at Ornans"? What a strange grouping of compositions in my head!

All the figures on the walls of the Carmine have dignity: Christ, the Apostles, St. Peter, even the beggars and cripples. Everyone is human. One memorable figure of a begger-mother holding her child is ultimate in its simplicity. The colors—browns, reds, yellows, greens—all muted (by time?), are intrinsic to the content and add to the overall humanity and warmth. But more than man's dignity is expressed here; one sees his vulnerability too: the grief of Adam and Eve expelled from Eden, the misery of beggars and cripples, the shivering bodies of people being baptized, all without a trace of sentimentality. And somewhere in the background of these compositions there lurks a brilliant young face with an energetic and restless expression, believed to be Masaccio himself.

In Rome, Florence, Naples, Vienna and Paris are Caravaggio's paintings of saints' miracles and tortures, of madonnas, of Christ, and of the Virgin's death. The characters in these nominally religious pictures are mostly poor, barefoot, ragged people. Unlike Masaccio's murals, Caravaggio's are theatrical compositions in which the figures are arranged like the dramatis personae in a play, where the action and gestures are determined by the director. Caravaggio's great restraint and tempestuous emotion produce tremendous energy, like a welding of Delacroix and Courbet, romanticism and realism combined. The fantastic virility of his draftsmanship beggars description. Everything is full of movement, pulsates and heaves with life: faces, shoulders, arms and hands, thumbs, veins in the ankles. His people are as real as the men and women in the paintings of Louis Le Nain. It interests me to find his frequent juxtaposition of youth and age, an energetic, smooth-browed face of a young woman next to an old wrinkled one.

These artists who died so young—Masaccio, Caravaggio, Géricault, Van Gogh, Seurat—fulfilled themselves. One need not bewail their short lives. But imagine if Titian, Rembrandt, or Degas had died at the age of Masaccio and Caravaggio! They needed long life. It is tragic only when artists live long without excelling, or even equalling their early achievements. But these too should be recognized and honored, even if they produce nothing else.

August 1, 1966

Before leaving Italy, we were invited by John and Alice Rewald to drive with them to Lucca. Alice was the skilled chauffeur and John the anxious navigator. We visited the home of Herbert Handt, the tenor, and his wife, Laura

Ziegler, the sculptor, who a year ago made an excellent likeness of me in terra cotta, the way I am now, dentured and sunken-eyed. From Lucca, we went to Pietra Santa to the Fonderia d'Arte of Vignale and Tomaso, a foundry with a traditional reputation for skillful casting. Sculptors of various persuasions, academic, avant-garde, and everything in between, bring their work to be cast there. They also work there, in one tremendous common studio, indoors as well as in the open. The man most respected by the sculptors and casters at this time is seventy-five-year-old Jacques Lipchitz. We found him that morning working in the yard on one of his mythological compositions, a huge entanglement of figures, human and animal. In his beret and smock he looked like a sculptor, vigorous, generous in body, full-faced, sun-tanned, his gray hair picturesquely untrimmed. His welcome was warm and friendly, his speech peculiarly his own, intermingled with French, English, Russian, Yiddish. I've always liked Lipchitz's appearance, his voice, the fusion of sophistication and folksy intelligence in him. He was most gracious that day, introduced us to the sculptors and casters and to the extraordinary proprietor of the foundry, Luigi Tomaso, whom

36

Jacques Lipchitz

everyone calls "Mama Gigi" because he's so helpful and solicitous of everyone's needs. We had an excellent lunch with him and Lipchitz in a simple, rustic setting which they said was a workers' club.

After lunch we went to Lipchitz's studio where we saw the plaster model of his monument to Duluth, a French explorer who founded the city in Minnesota that bears his name. (Now I'm not quite certain of the name of that picturesque explorer, nor of the city. I had so much wine and good food that afternoon. Shall I try to check it, or just leave it at that?) But I do remember the imaginative quality and animation of that carnival-like figure attired in an eighteenth-century costume, plumed hat, gauntlets and all. Jacques Lipchitz told us he had no likenesses to follow, but had to base his portrait only on verbal descriptions in old documents.

In the studio there was also a large, unfinished plaster cast of Hagar and Ishmael. "I did this," Lipchitz said, gesturing vaguely, ". . . the idea is friendship between Arabs and Jews in Israel . . . an idea . . ." Lipchitz is one of those artists who are able to use mythological and biblical themes for plastic interpretation of contemporary events and concerns.

August 4, 1966

Now that I am engaged in writing this, I find that some early memories appear more vivid, in the literal sense of the word "appear." They come out of the deep recesses of my mind, like the incident of the dead infant with the tail between his legs. Some later memories are not so concrete.

Our arrival in America is vague in my memory. It seems that we landed in Philadelphia, where our father left the six of us and our mother to stay with her relatives, while he went to New York to find employment as a teacher of Hebrew.

We had Rembrandt eyes, all of us, father, mother and children (except Isaac), heavy-lidded, soft, brown. The eyes of the two youngest, Rebecca and Israel, were huge, icon-like. They loomed big in their little faces. Isaac's eyes were different. He had Dürer eyes, but brown, not blue. There is a painting in the Alte Pinakothek in Munich, of one Oswalt Krell, by Dürer, that always makes me think of Isaac when he was a child, and even now, when I saw it, although it's a portrait of a man, it brought to my mind vividly how Isaac looked when we were in Philadelphia, thin, intense, nervous. Seven or eight at that time, he was deeply religious, fanatically so—one of those inexplicable, mysterious phases of childhood. His behavior and moods were unrelated to those of the other children in that household of brothers, sisters, cousins. He prayed continuously, and when he prayed he seemed to be in a trance. One could do anything to him in those moments: pinch him, tickle him, slap him, lift him and carry him about the room, as our brutish, much older cousin would do. He would not interrupt his prayers, although his Dürer, but brown, eyes would blink angrily. Only when he finished would he strike out at his tormentors, curse and cry.

Moses and I were humiliated and angry when all five of us, even our little sister, were put in the same class of a Philadelphia public school. In Borisoglebsk we had just been admitted to the *gymnasia*, wore brass-badged hats and uniforms, and were already steeped in Russian literature, having read all the adult books in our father's library. We also knew, in Russian translation, *The Prince and the Pauper, Uncle Tom's Cabin*, and the novels of Charles Dickens and Thackeray. *Uncle Tom's Cabin* I knew almost by heart, having read it so many times to my as yet unlettered, but intelligent and compassionate younger brother, Isaac. The trials and sorrows of Uncle Tom and the death of little white Eva never failed to make him shed silent tears, and my voice, too, would tremble with emotion. In the *gymnasia* my compositions on Lomonosov (the Russian Benjamin Franklin), and Turgenev's *A Hunter's Sketches* and other books, were beginning to be read to the class by the teacher.

Moses at that time was considered somewhat of a mathematical wizard. He could multiply and divide any large numbers in his head. Also he was known to have surpassed his teacher in drawing. I still remember a pen and ink drawing by this teacher, of a boat in turbulent waters, given to Moses with the inscription: "To my favorite pupil."

And now here we were in a classroom with babies!

Nevertheless, during the several months of our stay in Philadelphia, Moses and I were often able to forget our advanced age, our sophistication, forget that we were foreigners, and in spite of the language barrier lost our self-consciousness and joined in schoolyard activities. It was only after we came to New York that we found ourselves suddenly plunged into a strange world. We ceased to be children and withdrew.

But in Philadelphia we were still children. We played, roamed the streets of the city, had encounters with native kids and defended ourselves when attacked. These were normal, boyish experiences.

Moses was the daring and assertive one. In the schoolyard, when a bully finally got Moses's goat by constantly picking on us, he suddenly hurled himself on our tormentor without warning. In a matter of seconds there was a cloud of dust, scattered pencils, books, even shoes, and a prostrate boy.

Once, while exploring an unknown neighborhood, we were accosted by a gang of jeering, hostile boys. It didn't take long for a fight to develop. Moses fought valiantly, but as for me, I must confess that I did not strike out, not even to defend myself, but let a boy jump on me and pull me down. Dazedly I was conscious of a pleasant sensation, and I somehow felt that the boy on top of me experienced the same satisfaction. After a while we disengaged ourselves and ran, with our "enemies" in pursuit. When we reached safety and the gasping, breathless little Isaac caught up with us, Moses declared, "*Nu, 'Volka boiatsia v lies nie khodit,'*" which means, "Well, 'he who fears wolves should not venture into the forest,'" a Russian proverb which served as a slogan for us.

August 6, 1966

Though I often question the value of what I am doing, I find it delightful to involve myself in writing, in authorship. For me there is no competition here, no professional standard. It is an escape from my confusing, choleric world of

39

art. When I was young and became unhappy with my paintings and drawings, when I thought I was not living up to my then naïve, grandiose expectations, I would seek escape in any routine job—as an all-around boy in a shop, a dishwasher in an ice cream parlor, an embroidery worker—and find relief. Now I find similar relief in writing these lines.

Often, when traveling between France and Italy, we stop in the rather dull and stodgy city of Basel just to see the Holbeins again. I am always intrigued and impressed by the personalities of the great artists, Masaccio, Vermeer, Degas, Van Eyck, Cézanne, Seurat, Brueghel, Rembrandt, Renoir. I like to take them out of their historical context. I wish there were a book written from that point of view. Then perhaps one could come closer to an understanding of what genius is. For those I mentioned are out of sequence of time and events.

Holbein was so unlike his German contemporaries—serene, gestureless, grimaceless. I'm referring to his portraits, which are monuments, rather than paintings, images for eternity. My favorite Holbein is the portrait of his wife and children, truthful, non-flattering, so tangible that you can smell the baby. This mother and her children are not medieval; they are out of time.

The top floor of this museum is filled with more recent and contemporary art, beginning with the French Impressionists. There is an interesting self-portrait of Cézanne, well-groomed, almost beguiling, a small canvas of a three-quarter view, unlike his other self-portraits which are mainly of a dishevelled head.

Then there are rooms filled with the work of European Expressionists, Munch, Kokoschka, extraordinary, late paintings by Corinth, some Beckmanns, an excellent group of Chagalls; one youthful and one mature painting by Picasso—"Two Brothers," a naked young boy carrying his little naked brother on his back, and a still-life of a brown, drop-leaf table with a bowl of fruit. This is followed by rooms of Légers, Braques, Juan Gris', and the many inevitable Paul Klees, Kandinskys, Mirós and . . . pandemonium: pop art, op art, kinetic and mobile art. We were amused by two American paintings, a typical Mark Rothko in brown, red and white, and a Barnett Newman, also typical, I suppose: a tall panel of navy-blue with a sky-blue strip on top and bottom. One was called factually, "Brown, Red and White," while the other was pretentiously entitled, "The Day Before One."

"Why not call the Barnett Newman 'The Day After Tomorrow?'" my wife said, and laughed.

Paris—August 10, 1966

I am one of the older people walking along Boulevard Saint Germain. My hair is white and I'm aware that Paris is a city of and for young people. What an abundance of thighs and legs! Apparently young women would like to go about naked, or at least in bikinis.

It's August, and Paris is in its full beauty. It's the beginning of fall, the season of *listopad* (in Russian, the "falling of leaves"). At this time of year the planned vistas are unmarred by traffic. How can one describe adequately the beauty, the esthetic wealth of this city, so filled to the brim with art?

As soon as we arrived we took a walk through the gracious gardens of the Tuileries, and found ourselves in the Orangerie where we saw a profusion of Cézannes, Renoirs, Utrillos, Rousseaus, Picassos, Derains, Matisses, Soutines and Modiglianis, the collection of Paul Guillaume. Again an evidence of how rich France is in art. It has produced many great painters and adopted many more from other countries; their work fills the museums of the world. I am poignantly reminded now of something that Yasuo Kuniyoshi wrote about himself in some publication a long time ago. He described his stay in Paris, how he worked there, how much he liked it and thought of remaining, but in the end he decided to return to New York because, as he said, "France is so rich in art and artists, and America so poor." He wanted to contribute to the art of his adopted country.

As always the Louvre overwhelmed me. Again I was held by Delacroix's "Liberty Leading the People" and "The Massacre at Scio"; by Courbet's

"Studio" and "Burial at Ornans." These great canvases humble and inspire me. In front of the "Burial" I found myself muttering to myself, "What a painting, what a painting!"

August 18, 1966

Our stay in Paris was made more interesting by a friend who took us on a trip through the small towns outside the city: Argenteuil, Pontoise and others, the names of which I can't recall. This is the locale where Pissarro, Sisley, Monet, Renoir and Cézanne painted their landscapes that became so well known and loved. Their motifs are still recognizable both in the canvases on the walls of the Jeu du Paume and in the locales themselves, in spite of the changes wrought by time and civilization. There are modern factories there.

The high point of this pilgrimage was Auvers, the town where Van Gogh worked at the end of his life and where he shot himself. His spirit still permeates this suburb of Paris. There is a café now in the house where he lived— or was it there then too? On the top floor is his room, small, stony, a dormer window near the ceiling, a narrow iron bedstead, an old, worn-out chair, an 1890 calendar on the wall. The austerity of it! A prison cell! I thought of his paintings, of his life. What tragedy and triumph.

We went to the cemetery where we found two simple tombstones side by side, one saying, "*Ici repose Vincent Van Gogh,*" and the other, "*Ici repose Théodore Van Gogh,*" with only the dates on each of his birth and death.

I stopped short at the sight of the fields around the cemetery. I felt a sharp pang; they were exactly like Van Gogh's last paintings in their flatness, shape and expanse. The time of day was different, the season may have been different, there were no big blackbirds at the moment, but this was unmistakably Van Gogh's landscape.

In a small old park we found Zadkine's monument to Van Gogh, a Don

Zadkine's Monument
to Van Gogh

Quixotish figure. Did Zadkine mean to imply that Van Gogh was another Don Quixote?

Though it was getting late, I made a quick, inadequate drawing in my battered sketchbook. Some young boys, giggling and making comments, were watching. I said to one, "*Asseyez-vous, s'il vous plaît*," pointing to the base of the statue, and sketched him in below Van Gogh's figure. Then I said, "*Merci*," and we shook hands. I gave him my pencil and said, "*Nom?*" He wrote: "TRIQUET." "*Qui est le sculpteur?*" I asked. All the boys ran out to read the name on the plaque outside the gate of the park and came back calling out in unison: "Zadkine!" Talking all at once, they were telling me now about Van Gogh, a "*peintre fameux*," his room, the cemetery, and so on.

43

We cut our stay in Paris short by a few days to visit the Rewalds in their medieval La Citadelle in Menerbes, in the Vaucleuse region of southern France. Our first stop was Autun to see the Nativity by the Master of Moulins. I have loved that picture ever since I first saw a color reproduction of it in one of the Skira books. With its delicate figure of the Virgin in blue and white it looked like an enlarged early French illumination (though, of course, one cannot generally judge color from the usual jazzed-up reproductions). To my disappointment, the Nativity was not there at the moment, but at The Hague, in an exhibition called "In the Light of Vermeer." (This was not tragic, for we were to catch up with it at The Hague the next week.)

Anyway, our visit to Autun was not a total loss, for in the medieval, turreted cathedral towering above this ancient little town, I found the "Martyr-

44

A Saint in Autun

dom of St. Sophronia" by Ingres, a large composition, densely crowded with dramatic figures and faces. I knew this painting from reproductions, as well as the many complete and detailed studies for it of heads, groups of figures nude and robed, and of gesturing hands.

Next day John Rewald came for us in Avignon in his car driven by Joseph, the caretaker of his place.

"Where is Alice?" we asked, disappointed. It's Alice who usually drives John around.

"There's a fête in the village tomorrow, and Alice took Victoria, Joseph's daughter, to buy her new shoes."

After the cold spell of Paris and Autun, we were grateful for the sunniness of that afternoon. John was in high spirits, which rose higher the closer we got to his Citadelle in Menerbes. Continuously he pointed out the picturesqueness of the area and extolled the fertility of the land, and he hummed buoyantly to himself as we drove along in the open car, enveloped by the warm wind.

Eve—in Autun

45

"Menerbes is on the other side of the mountain," he said, pointing to a range of hills. "Now hold your breath," he said after a while, "we're approaching it." And there was La Citadelle, with its tower, the highest point of the village.

We were amazed at the comfortable, modern renovation, or rather reconstruction, of the interior of this ancient fortress. The triangular shape of the grounds is like a miniature Vert Gallant, not under a bridge on the Seine to be sure, but high on a mountain. From this height one could see the tiled roofs and steep narrow streets of the stony village. The landscape of vineyards and farmland surrounded by mountains was beyond description. It was breathlessly spacious. I was confused: was it Cézanne? Piero della Francesca?

In renovating the house, the Rewalds utilized its original architecture and medieval oddities. The master bathroom in the tower is like a Guggenheim Museum, with its white, round walls and domed ceiling. There were even appropriate pictures on the walls, a Pascin drawing of a nude with spread thighs, as only he could do. From every aperture and window one could see the controlled profusion of colorful flowers and trees in the garden around the house. John was as proud of this garden as of the panoramic view and of La Citadelle with its rare furniture and objets d'art chosen with knowledgeable effort.

How unusual it is, Rebecca thought, for this urbane and famous art historian to be so absorbed in flowering plants and trees. He applies his esthetics to them, making color combinations of various flowers, harmonious and exotic.

The next day Alice Rewald gave a party. A group of people came, none of them natives of the region, all members of some kind of an international intelligentsia: Madame de Staël, a neighbor in Menerbes; Julien Levy, the former art dealer and biographer of Arshile Gorky, and his wife; the artist Bernard Pfriem, who has been summering in the nearby village of Lacoste for many years; his nextdoor neighbor, an English painter and friend of mine, Peter de Francia; a French winner of the Nobel Prize in biology, Professor Lwoff, whose mother posed for Serov, the famous Russian painter.

In a good mood because of several drinks, I talked with pleasurable ease in Russian to the Professor. He paints too, he told me, and likes to make pictures of the East River when he visits New York. From a window, I surmised, high up, from a bird's eye view, not like me who painted it close at hand in the late twenties.

But really it was not the liquor but the warmth and charm of Alice Rewald that put me, a stranger to this multilingual, worldly group, at ease.

I wandered through the rooms of La Citadelle and found myself in John's study, his "office," as he calls it. In a bookcase which took up an entire wall were Rewald's *History of Impressionism*, and *History of Post-Impressionism*, in several languages and editions, also his works on Cézanne, Degas, Maillol, Pissarro and others. On the table were more books on Cézanne by different authors in German, English and French, probably references for his forthcoming definitive book on the life and art of this great painter. I leafed through one of these books and was pleased to find a reproduction of a drawing made by Cézanne of Murillo's painting, "Little Beggar Boy," which is in the Louvre and which I've always been fond of.

A sketch of Alice by Kokoschka, a pen and ink nude by Guttuso, were on the wall, and, of all things, a battered oil painting, meagerly framed, of Gauguin's two squatting Tahitian women.

"What's that?" I exclaimed to John as he came into the room.

"That's a copy of the Gauguin in the Jeu de Paume," he answered.

"Who did it?"

"I committed it," John answered.

I laughed as I realized that he used the word "committed" advisedly.

The Rewalds took us to see Lacoste, a smaller, even stonier village, poorer and more primitive than Menerbes. Adding to the gloomy beauty of this place is the ruined castle of the Marquis de Sade. Originally a fortress, it was rebuilt in the seventeenth century as a luxurious chateau for the noble de Sade family. Now only zigzag ruins of stone walls remain. Like the Rewald's La Citadelle, it commands the Cézanne-Piero della Francesca view from the mountaintop.

Macabre platitudes filled my mind. How perishable everything is! Will the same happen in time to La Citadelle, so cleverly transformed and modernized, with its Vert Gallant triangle and its colorful flower arrangement, its furniture and objets d'art, its Guggenheim Museum bathroom? *Vanitas vanitatis*, all is vanity.

September 2, 1966

For some reason, I have no great interest in sculpture. I have made a few sporadic attempts at it, with little result. Often I even forget to look at it when I visit a museum. But I can become spellbound by an Egyptian, Gothic or Romanesque figure, and I am in awe of the sculpture of Michelangelo, Donatello and Rodin. During this trip, however, I was glad to see the lifework of two sculptors, the Giacometti exhibition in Basel and the work of Bourdelle in the Paris museum that bears his name.

I had previously seen a Giacometti retrospective in the Museum of Modern Art in New York, selected and edited to the point of preciousness and sterility. (Why does the Museum of Modern Art at times so dehumanize its one-man shows? It had once an exhibition of De Chirico where nothing but his metaphysical street scenes were shown, none of his self-portraits or figure compositions, making it monotonous and gloomy.)

For the first time, at the Giacometti exhibition in Basel, I warmly responded to the work of this limited and obsessed man. It was a huge, all-inclusive, diverse show, from talented youthful drawings, paintings and sculpture, naïve and fresh, to the very last repetitious, fleshless and sexless figures, striding or standing still. There was a large group of his mature paintings, predominantly in slate gray touched with yellow, red, or some other color, lava-like in texture from having been painted, scratched, scraped and painted again many times. His abstract, experimental and surrealistic bronzes which were given such prominence in the Museum of Modern Art show, were here shown in their proper context. From this all-inclusive show I did get the feeling of a rare, searching, non-competitive and altogether humble artist and man.

Before leaving for Europe, I read James Lord's book, a poetic account of how he posed for Giacometti. What trials and frustrations they both went through! Unbelievable! And judging from the reproduction in the book, the painting remained unfinished. But Giacometti never considered any of his work finished or completely realized. I can imagine the painter who did the Frick portrait of Philip IV in three sittings in a makeshift studio under unfavorable conditions, saying, after reading Mr. Lord's book: "What's all the fuss about? It's only a simple portrait."

Yet I left the show in Basel with a greater understanding of the work of Giacometti. I felt that in its frustration and obsession, even in its limitations, there is something redeeming.

A good way to describe Bourdelle's work is to say that it is entirely opposite that of Giacometti—loud, huge, lusty, rhetorical and dramatic. There is no searching, experimenting, or frustration here: it is confident, strong, imaginative, and staggeringly skillful. The portraits of himself, of Rodin, of Anatole France, the beautiful heads and figures of Juno-esque women, the deeply expressive madonna and child, are inspired.

But I really went to the Bourdelle Museum to see the exhibition of drawings of Isadora Duncan by Segonzac and Bourdelle, plus a few by some others, notably Rodin. These were all as good as one would expect from artists of such stature, and they did evoke some of the spirit of Isadora's dancing. Personally, I was sorry there were none of the numerous watercolors of Isadora by another of her devoted admirers, the American painter Abraham Walkowitz.

As part of her program to bring back to public attention the work of painters who, for whatever reason, become neglected and forgotten even during their lifetime, Virginia Zabriskie recently put on a small posthumous exhibition of watercolors and drawings by Abraham Walkowitz. His work always made me think of what Chekhov said of his own early stories: "I wrote them completely without effort, as a bird sings."

I think Walkowitz never worked hard on paintings. There was no effort in them. He never attempted themes demanding much grappling with content

Abraham Walkowitz

and technique. His work was always youthful, colorful and cheerful. It has its own profoundness.

This show was mostly of New York before the first world war, with a few scenes prophetic of the megalopolis that it has become. Even these are disarming, and lyrical, so unlike the dynamic watercolors of New York by Walkowitz's contemporary, Marin.

I first met Walkowitz in the middle twenties, over forty years ago, in an obscure little club of writers and artists called the Jewish Art Center. Who sent me there I no longer remember. I came with a few small, tentative pictures which I had brought back from a month's painting in Gloucester. Diffidently I showed them to the artists who were present. Among them was the buoyant, stocky little Walkowitz, who looked at my work and said, "Say, he'll be an artist." A still smaller man, a hunchback with a constantly emotional face, nodded approvingly. Later I learned that he was Jennings Tofel, who, together with Benjamin Kopman, was one of the initiators of this group. Slight though it was, this was my first professional recognition, and I still feel deeply grateful to these two men, for I was very shy then, and young, not in years (I don't remember myself ever having been young in years) but in any kind of experience and social behavior.

I was accepted as a member of this club. The pictures were exhibited and immediately sold for ten or fifteen dollars apiece. One was a small oil on Beaverboard, of a street after a rain, the sunset reflected in a puddle, with a sailor and his girl walking away in the distance and a boy peeing against a fence. Another oil showed a façade of a Gloucester frame house, with women and children sitting on the stoop or climbing the outside stairway. Two or three watercolors of similar subject matter were also sold. I wonder where these pictures are now, or if they still exist.

I believe that by the time I met Walkowitz he was no longer painting; at any rate, I never knew him to have a studio. For many years he would complain of his failing eyesight, but he would still get around, see exhibitions, look at pictures, praise or criticize them, discuss art at great length. Finally he did lose his sight, and then this charming, rosy-faced, white-haired old artist, who was seen for years on 57th Street, in museums, at concerts, and dance recitals, dropped out of the artistic scene of New York.

But about two years before his death, Walkowitz finally had a bit of gratification; he was recognized and honored by his peers. At a meeting of a committee for grants and awards of the American Institute of Arts and Letters, I suggested that he be considered for the special award that is granted to an older artist. A restrained discussion followed. Some said other artists were more worthy; one opinion was that this was not meant to be a charity award to a needy artist, but recognition for accomplishment; still others that Walkowitz had stopped being an artist since he hadn't painted for many years. To all this I replied that it was unjust to forget the early contributions to American art of men who in their later years became inactive for various reasons: illness, discouragement, disillusionment. I cited the names of authors, composers, and painters of other countries who are honored for even a single creative work in their lifetime.

That May ceremonial of the Institute was memorable. It was dramatically moving to see the old, blind, white-haired Abraham Walkowitz led to the platform for his award, to the acclaim and standing ovation of the audience.

Later, probably the last time I saw him, Walkowitz told me that the award came too late.

That was an inbred group at the Jewish Art Center—proud, touchy, self-conscious and pretentious in its Jewishness. The painters wrote, the writers were involved in painting. Both Tofel and Kopman wrote books à la Nietzsche, and painted mystical and confused pictures. Tofel's canvases were poetic, nebulous in color and drawing, compositions of dwarfed, religiously posturing people.

The glamorous figure of the Jewish Art Center was Benjamin Kopman. No one questioned his talent. He was virile, wiry, handsome, curly-headed. In 1963, about two years before he died, I saw him at an opening of his exhibition, frail, but distinguished looking. His art was intense and personal, but affected by a number of tendencies prevalent during his lifetime. His earliest work, for instance, which I vaguely remember, had a "Munich school" look, popular then in this country. Later there was a Ryder-ish quality, and then a number of influences: Rousseau, Chagall, Rouault. Towards the end, when his art mellowed, as often happens with older artists, it assumed the quality of a sort of German expressionism, but gentle and benign. His own gifts, however, his integrity and intensity, endowed his painting with individual worth. There was something tragic in Kopman. His shy pride, his reticence and his withdrawal limited his milieu to a circle of Yiddish intellectuals, poets, writers and actors who admired him and in whose parochial acceptance he allowed himself to bask.

My wife and I attended Benjamin Kopman's quiet and humble funeral. By a strange coincidence, there appeared in that day's *New York Times Magazine* a long, elaborate and well-illustrated article on Marc Chagall, entitled "Little Boy from Vitebsk Makes Good." Vitebsk was also the birthplace of Kopman, and he was born the same year as Chagall. Two painters from the same world and era, but what different lives and fates!

Chagall well deserves his great fame. Whenever I see an early painting of his, I marvel. What a medley of Jewish and Russian life and lore, reality and fantasy, Sholem Aleichem, Gogol . . . What were *his* influences? Certainly not traditional ones. Is he what the Russians call a *samorodock*, that is, born of himself? Is he really naïve or is he sophisticated? Shrewd or simple? In old Russian culture, folk religion, there were the "holy simpletons" who were endowed with a mystic and prophetic talent. Is Chagall one of art's "holy simpletons," like Rousseau, for instance? But then he's also Cubist, Surrealist, Expressionist. I'd better not become too involved here. He is a phenomenon.

September 4, 1966

====

We caught up finally with the Master of Moulins. His "Adoration of the Shepherds" at The Hague exhibition, "In the Light of Vermeer," was as beautiful as I had imagined it.

It's wonderful to be in a room full of Vermeers, with the miraculous "View of Delft" and the "Turbaned Girl," but for me the great single painting was the De La Tour. It is called "The Virgin and St. Anne," and again is one of those nominally religious pictures that fascinate me, of two women by candlelight, tenderly watching a swaddled baby.

We stood in line for half an hour waiting to get into the Museum. With what loving attention the visitors studied these modest paintings centuries removed from them! So unlike the viewers at the various *Biennales* where nothing is for study, scrutiny and contemplation. Did I say centuries removed?

There were also paintings by Corot, Degas and Cézanne. They held their own in the company of the older masters. How timeless great art is!

Amsterdam — September 12, 1966

For me, Holland is Rembrandt, yet nothing I saw in Holland recalled Rembrandt's paintings.

This is our last day in Amsterdam. In the morning I went back to the Rijksmuseum, to take one last look at the Rembrandts. Once there, I just had to stop and make a quick sketch of a figure in "Adoration of the Kings" by Geertgen Tot St. Jans. I love that painter of plain, awkward people; of women with retroussé noses; of simple colors, rose, brown, tan and black. Then I spent the rest of the time in front of the "Jewish Bride," "The Syndics," the "Questioning St. Peter," and Rembrandt's self-portrait as St. Paul.

54

Figure from Geertgen Tot St. Jans

Yesterday a friend of ours took us in her car to the Zuyder Zee country. The small towns which we passed through were like paintings by Heyden and Berckheyde, only more beautiful now with age. Time has weathered the bricks, tilted the equilibrium of the houses, and buckled their walls. Only the cars create a disturbance; here, like everywhere else, they destroy space and perspective.

It was a typical September day in Holland, with rapidly moving clouds and intermittent sunshine. We passed pastures of grazing cattle, farms, canals. We got out of the car to look at cathedrals, into courtyards, even into windows of houses. Ruisdael, Van Goyen, Cuyp, Van de Velde, de Hooch and Terborch, even Saenredam and Vermeer (we saw a girl or two who looked like the "Turbaned Girl" in The Hague) came alive. But not Rembrandt. He is beyond time and place. We encountered no "Blind Homer," no "Jewish Bride," not even one of the "Syndics." In the homeless faces on Second Avenue I saw, many times, Rembrandt's self-portrait as St. Paul.

September 13, 1966

Soon after joining our father in New York, I destroyed the notebook containing my Russian poems. I tore it up, page by page, and flushed it down the toilet. They were written under the spell of the romantic, altruistic Nadson, and were about birds who lost their nests and about wandering children who had no homes. All the poems had quatrains added by my father to the effect: "Thus art thou, my people. Thou hast lost thy nest (or 'home,' as the case might be) but one day thou shalt find it, recapture it and return to it."

The last poem in that notebook was one I wrote shortly before leaving Borisoglebsk. It was not about birds or children any more. I described myself musing on the banks of the river Vorona, watching its flow carrying heavy beams and stones, and asking it why it was unable to carry away my heavy thoughts. It was without my father's quatrain.

55

When our father ushered us all into the apartment he had rented in the South Bronx, our mother said, reproachfully, "Are these the rooms? They look like closets."

The same pattern of disappointments she experienced all her life. And a succession of our father's failures. I'm not implying our father was a failure; it was simply that his concrete accomplishments somehow never measured up to his talents. He was a naïve romantic who was not able to realize his hopes. He was childishly uncompromising, unable to cope with the inconsistencies of his world. He did not even grasp the turbulent inner life of our bewildered mother, bewildered by the children who came one after another when she was still so young, by her inability to cope with them as they grew, by the void in her own intellectual growth, the realization of which made her alternately angry and melancholy.

London—September 14, 1966

We're in London. The tree outside the window of our hotel is rustling in the wind. In two weeks we'll be on the ship taking us back to New York, my world, my country. I must hurry. I want to end this compulsive writing.

Our father changed. He now had a trim goatee, his hair was gray, his cheeks hollow. There was a feverish look in his heavy-lidded eyes. His voice was hoarse from outshouting his unruly pupils. He coughed. He wrote no more in his beloved Hebrew, but turned to commercial writing for the Yiddish newspapers "to make a living."

Later, in a more spacious Bronx apartment, our mother let Moses, Isaac and myself have a room in which to draw and paint. On its glossy, cream-colored walls, we thumbtacked our drawings and nailed our earliest canvases. The disorder was indescribable. We were almost adults. Cramped, restless and irritable, we got into one another's way and quarreled.

Artist's Mother

Dancing Lesson

Isaac

Isaac, the youngest of us three, often amazed me with his talent. When, several years later, I needed a back view of myself for one of my first compositions, a subway scene, it was Isaac I asked to make a drawing of me holding on to an imaginary subway strap. He did just what I wanted. I copied it onto the canvas, and had only to fill in the greenish gray of the long coat and the brown of the beat-up hat.

Moses and I became increasingly and painfully aware of the special problem of being twins who had the same interests and attitudes, which tended to make our paintings look alike. When the time arrived, on Moses' initiative we decided to go to different art schools. He enrolled in the then fascinating school at the Educational Alliance on the East Side, I in the more traditional National Academy. Isaac hesitated between the two, attended the Academy for a while, then left for the Alliance.

We neglected our academic studies, though Isaac did finish high school. Fannie, the sister closest to us in years, became absorbed in mastering the English language and going to college. I do not remember much contact with the two

57

younger children at that time; we loved them as older children love their younger siblings, without understanding them. We were so young ourselves. Nor do I know how much attention our parents, in their own daily turmoil, were able to give them.

I am here writing about my brothers and sisters in the years of their own growth, which they surely remember themselves. They may question what I say. But these are my memories.

The patriarchal quality of our family living came to an end. Everyone became involved with himself. I entered into a long period of fog from which I emerged only at intervals. I functioned after a fashion, I went to art schools and took on jobs. At home, of course, I felt more at ease and constantly drew the immediate members of my family, which now included our grandmother. She would sit in a rocking chair under our mother's large rubber plants, like an Henri Rousseau painting.

But I withdrew almost completely from other social contacts. Whenever the doorbell rang I would run off to my room. Harassed though he was himself, my father noticed this strange behavior and tried, in his way, to shame me out of it. He would say, "Hurry, hide under the table; Dominic the ice man is coming in." I rarely talked, and perhaps my persistent Russian accent and low voice can be traced back to this period. I simply didn't give my vocal cords enough exercise.

I neglected my appearance. I took long, lonely walks. Barbers standing in their doorways on the Bowery would beckon to me, trying to persuade me to submit to a haircut. Jeeringly they would say, "For nothing." Smart-alecky kids would stop me in my most withdrawn moments and ask, "Hey, where's the nearest barber shop?" Bewildered, I would look around to find one, much to their amusement.

My mind was filled with fantasies. I was a kind of Walter Mitty, imagining myself in flamboyant roles, a great painter, a poet, even a strong man or acrobat. But any slight happening would jolt me back into my anxious reality. Once, on such a trance-like walk, I found myself following a boy my age who was walking jauntily, carelessly. Before I realized what I was doing I began to imitate him, became youthful, carefree and skipped along like him. Suddenly I caught myself and felt shamed and embarrassed at playing a part out of character.

I stopped. I still can see my dim reflection in the dark glass of the store window, stooped, unkempt, slinking away.

Moses was the first of the brothers to bring friends into the house, boys and girls. Our mother greeted these young art students warmly and became fond of them. Young Chaim Gross, a picturesque, penniless foreigner from Galicia's Carpathian hills, came and was welcomed. Louis Riback, a native East Side kid, both tough and sensitive, was a frequent visitor. But the youngest, handsomest and most precocious of all was the talented, red-haired Peter Blume.

My brothers and I saw a great deal of Chaim. Time had a different property then—there seemed so much of it. We spent long summer days together in City Island, Pelham Bay and Spuyten-Duyvil, then undeveloped and picturesque, more like outskirts of New York. Chaim was a curious product of the first world war: unlettered, his normal education neglected, but rich in native intelligence, and talented. On these outings we took along our sketch pads and watercolors. We would swim in the Hudson, row in Pelham Bay and draw and paint landscapes. Chaim's watercolors had a semi-wild flavor. I became critically aware of how accurate and tame mine were in comparison with his imaginative, expressionistic ones.

Peter Blume soon left our group, becoming a celebrated painter before he was twenty. He went off to Connecticut and began to paint sophisticated, neo-primitive pictures of New England which seemed extraordinary, beyond my understanding at that time. He was far ahead of us with such complex, composite paintings as "Parade" and "South of Scranton." A few years later I was overwhelmed by his "Eternal City." Even today when I look at it in the Museum of Modern Art I marvel at the skill, the persistence which went into the making of this unique composition.

Once Moses came with a pretty, plump girl, Eugenie Silverman, and later our mother cried when she looked out of the window and saw her oldest son go off with a girl for the first time.

Beyla (we called our mother Beyla now, father Avrohom) would often come into our room. One day while she was quietly watching us work, the telephone rang. Someone called to say that Leo Jakenson had drowned. Our mother began to cry in her silent manner. The whole family was attached to this friend of Moses, a strange, slight, elusive fellow. Moses and I were almost in awe of him. He was our age, but far advanced in art. In our eyes he was already a master. His work even attracted the attention of Robert Henri and George Bellows, the two socially minded leaders in American art at that time. With skill and understanding extraordinary for his age, he painted life-size portraits of the East Side people who posed in the school. Death became a reality—a contemporary had died.

His thin, inconsolable mother, began to visit us after his death to talk with Beyla. Upon leaving our house she would invariably stumble over the last few steps because her vision was blurred by tears.

When I entered the life class at the National Academy for the first time, I was as overwhelmed by the work of the students as Gogol's hick, Vacula, was when he came to Moscow. In my untutored and inexperienced eyes, their work seemed as wonderful to me as pictures by Velásquez and Frans Hals. After a while this initial excitement and amazement wore off, for I soon realized that art is more than skillful imitation of nature. One by one these able fellows received medals and prizes and immediately plunged into obscurity.

But there were others, restless, searching, dissatisfied with their drawings and paintings, who were not cited for awards: Ben Shahn, as much involved with theorizing about art as with painting; a bright boy in knee pants named Mike Schapiro; the exuberant young Sol Wilson, interested in music as well as in painting; Paul Cadmus, Lewitin, Martha Rythers. There were even some Cézanne-ists among us. These heretics would walk out of the classroom whenever the instructors came to criticize. We were a class of young, neurotic, dedicated students dreaming of fame, so unlike the art classes of today that seem to be filled with elderly amateurs.

I must not forget to mention that when I entered the Academy, the life-size paintings of Jan Matulka, a recent student who was becoming known as an artist at that time, were hanging on the classroom walls. His name was still on the lips of the older students. We were thrilled one day when he appeared in our class. We asked him to criticize and correct our pictures, showing him greater deference than we did to our old teachers, Francis C. Jones and Charles C. Curran.

But I was fond of George W. Maynard. He was then in his eighties, and had the head of a Roman senator. George Luks painted a life-size portrait of him in some kind of ecclesiastical robes. Mr. Maynard came to class at irregular intervals. He would childishly spout at me a few Russian phrases, which he had picked up in his youth when he was a sailor he told me. One day he looked at one of my studies of the model and said, "Why don't you go ahead and finish it? Now. You're quite young and have lots of time, but not an ocean of time." To show how he employed the word "ocean," I would have to write it like this, O-C-E-A-N.

Then this ancient artist failed to appear. Some time later a tall, masculine woman came in with a palette and mumbled that George W. Maynard, her deceased husband, willed his palette to his class. The moment she left we snickered and joked, youthfully thoughtless of age, authority, even of death.

I lacked the ability to associate freely and naturally with my fellow students. Years later, when I unexpectedly met one of them and we reminisced, he told me that I was considered aloof, proud, snobbish. The truth was that I desperately wanted to be friends with them, but didn't know how.

During all this time I was aware of another art school. Students talked about its radicalism and its modernism. Great men taught there at one time or another—George Bellows, John Sloan, Max Weber. I longed to go there, but its fees, about $14 a month, were way beyond my means, in spite of my odd jobs. Then one day my uncle, who was interested in my progress, offered to pay three months' tuition for me at the Art Students League.

The League was livelier, freer, noisier, less orderly than the National Academy. Fellows and girls worked in the same classrooms together, and the students had the privilege of choosing their teachers and changing classes every month. George Luks and Kenneth Hayes Miller were the most popular teachers when I was there. Once I watched George Luks give a painting demonstration to his class. He was in his element, a little drunk and exhilarated. He painted a child from memory, talking to the image on the canvas as if it were alive. "Ah, you're coming, you little devil. I'm getting you now." He pressed the brushes so vigorously on the canvas that he broke the handles of two of them. We watched him in fascination. After he finished he ceremoniously presented the picture to the monitor of the class. Privately, I thought it was too much of a display.

Kenneth Hayes Miller was the most influential teacher at the League. He was long-nosed and grim-visaged, but had a kind smile. He taught some of my brilliant contemporaries—Peggy Baron, Reginald Marsh, Alex Brook, Kuniyoshi, Isabel Bishop, Edward Laning—with all of whom he had a continuing friendship and whom he influenced even after they became established artists. Years later, when I was posing for Alex Brook he said "You know, when Miller finishes criticizing a painting of yours, you feel like pushing your foot through it."

I joined the class of Guy Pène du Bois. He was the most unobtrusive of the teachers. I didn't know his standing in the art world, but somewhere I may have seen and liked one of his small genre paintings. Inarticulate and timid as I was in those days, I was able to establish a rapport with this red-faced, also essentially shy man, who looked at me with sarcastic attention from behind his thick glasses. Actually he made no attempt to teach me anything. I realize now that he was not what is known as an "involved" teacher. As a matter of fact, there was something slightly cynical about him, as if he had said to himself, "I can't teach anyone to be an artist, but I have to teach to make a living." I liked and respected him, and my work changed merely from being with him. In the National Academy I had learned to paint cleverly from models, like my older fellow students, à la Sargent and Chase, who were our standards then. But at the League I made a conscious effort to shake off all that I had learned at the Academy. When I left the League I isolated myself in my parents' house and began to paint my immediate environment in an altogether personal manner.

After I had left his class, I met du Bois at gatherings in the Whitney Club.

On one occasion he approached me and said in his friendly but sarcastic manner, "The trouble with you, Soyer, is that you don't drink enough." This has since been rectified.

Slowly I was coming out of my foggy existence. At infrequent intervals I would visit du Bois, overcoming my shyness in my desire to know him, and would show him the paintings I was doing. One day he said, "Take this one to the Daniel Gallery and tell them I sent you."

It was a 20×24 canvas, which I called the "Dancing Lesson," depicting our sister Rebbie teaching Moses to dance to the harmonica music of our youngest brother Israel, who was pictured sitting on the sofa with Avrohom and our grandmother. Near them, on a heavy rocker, sat Beyla with a Yiddish newspaper in her lap. On the floor was a flower-bordered rug. The light blue wall was embellished by an enlarged framed photograph, popular in those days, of our grandparents. Beyla's rubber plant was in the corner. This painting is now owned by Chaim Gross. One may call it naïve; it is flat, without chiaroscuro or attempt to create depth. I consider it significant in my development.

When I brought "Dancing Lesson" to the Daniel Gallery, unwrapped it and propped it up against the wall under paintings by Niles Spencer, Pascin, Preston Dickinson, Cikovsky, Kuniyoshi and Peter Blume, I felt a great joy, which I tried to suppress, at seeing that my work looked as good as any of those already well-known artists. I could hardly believe it. After a whispered conversation between Mr. Daniel and his haggard associate, Mr. Hartpence, I was told that when I had twelve such paintings I would be given a one-man show. It took me a year to paint those twelve pictures in my spare time, and I had my first show in 1929. I now considered myself a full-fledged painter.

I began to work in studios, at first sharing them with other young artists, but soon having my own, all of them on the Lower East Side.

Time is measurable in months when one is young. Half a year is a period long enough in which to change, to grow, even to succeed. I was in the process, a prolonged one, of leaving home. I saw everything around me with clear, young eyes.

A tallish, slim girl, Rebecca, who wore her red hair in braids like a crown around her head, made curtains for the windows in my studio. She was my sister Fannie's school friend, whom I used to see in our house in the days of my deepest withdrawal. She became my wife.

It may have been after my third one-man show that I was invited to teach at the Art Students League. It was during the Depression, and a whole new staff consisting of, among others, Yasuo Kuniyoshi, Reginald Marsh, Harry Sternberg, Wortman of the "Metropolitan Movies" in the old *World*, and myself, was being hired. I considered this altogether unexpected invitation to teach a great honor, but I accepted the job with trepidation, for I felt ill-equipped. I had some experience as a volunteer teacher at the old John Reed Art Club, but this new situation was in an established school with a great art-teaching tradition. I had no theories about how to teach, no formulas for making pictures.

For me painting has always been a matter of trial and error. Even now, when I approach a new canvas I feel as if I had never painted before. I had no rules for composing; I never could understand formal analyses of composition. I was ignorant of all color theory and of anatomy, and I had no knowledge of media other than the basic one of oil and turpentine. What kind of a teacher could I have been? What could I then have told William Kienbush, who was in my class at that time, when he asked me how to proceed with his work? I still remember his questioning look. To Corinne West, later known as Michael West, I remember saying, "You're too brilliant. You use color too strategically." Even now I don't quite understand what I meant by this. I could not cope with the more advanced students. I could not give them any positive guidance.

However, in retrospect I think I was helpful after a fashion. Now and then I would find a young student with an odd ambition to become a Vermeer, a Van Gogh or Kokoschka. If he had talent, whatever that may be, I would say, "Go to it. When one is young, everything is possible. It may lead you to discover yourself."

Like my teacher, Guy Pène du Bois, I've always felt that one cannot be taught to be an artist, especially today. Art has become individualized and capricious; temporary "innovations" have replaced standards and traditions. I do believe, however, that even now students can gain from contact with a man whose work they admire. They seem to learn by osmosis; there is a certain inner rapport between the teacher and student, and verbal communication may not even be necessary.

September 22, 1966

The Tate Gallery has been completely reorganized since I was last there two years ago. I must say they've done a good job of putting things in order, making it easy and pleasant to follow the continuity of English painting from its early times through Wilson Steer, Walter Richard Sickert, Augustus John, and then, a break. What follows is the "modern" section of the Gallery. Except for the paintings of Bacon and Lucien Freud, this is a collection of all forms of non-representationalism, including the latest art of the moment, "op," "pop," "kinetic" and "cop." To apply the word "modern" to art is bad enough, in my opinion, but this is even beyond that. It should be called "momentary" art, if it is art at all.

I spoke to a couple of younger painters here, who told me that galleries and museums are reluctant to exhibit figurative work, that ninety-nine percent of the art shown here is non-objective, and that representational artists are losing confidence. As one of them said, "Even those who think figuratively paint non-figuratively." How long will this liquidation of art continue? Until its extinction? What is the reason for it?

This summer I saw some of the Holbein inimitable portrait drawings. I saw the "Coronation of Napoleon" by David, battle scenes by Delacroix, genre paintings by Louis Le Nain and Pieter Brueghel. They were the recorders of history and of daily life, the reporters and photographers of their day. But what is the artist today? What the devil is his role?

Several months ago I took part in a symposium called "Alienation of the Modern Artist," with the subtitle, "Must the Artist Communicate with his

Public?" I here include my opening statement for that symposium, for it may answer some of the questions raised above.

I would like to express my reservations about the title of this symposium. They pertain to the word *alienation*, and to the phrase *modern artist*. The word *alienation* is being bandied about too much these days. I still don't know exactly what it means, and when I've asked people for a definition, I have never gotten a concise answer. Always there have been vague allusions to the various conditions of mankind. After thinking about it, however, I finally came to the conclusion that alienation has always been with us. There have always been alienated people, artists and writers among them. One calls to mind painters of any period: Leonardo, Uccello, Cézanne, Van Gogh, Soutine, Munch; writers such as Dostoevsky, Kafka, Camus, Genet. We see alienated individuals among us every day, in every walk of life. Yes, the artist of today is alienated; doubly so, as I shall try to explain later on. It is not the word itself that I object to, but its use, as though it were a new concept.

Now, the phrase *modern artist*. I'm a painter and not a historian, but once in a while I like to ponder about the phenomenon of art, its history and philosophy. I cannot understand the application of the word *modern* to art. The word suggests ephemerality and transitoriness. I can accept the term *modern* in clothing, in housing, in decoration. I can even accept the phrase *modern life*. But art in its essence cannot be characterized as *modern* or *non-modern*.

In preparation for this symposium, I looked into Sir Herbert Read's *A Concise History of Modern Painting*, and the preface immediately aroused my anger. He says there that "a comprehensive history of modern painting is not at present possible because such history has not yet reached the end of its development." (Though when I look at the end of this book and see reproductions of paintings by Scott, Grippa, Kline and Hartung, I question how much farther towards absurdity this art can lead and into what kind of history of what he calls "modern painting" it can develop.)

Later in the preface Read says that to write this history he had to exclude the work of the realistic painters of today. He does not deny the accomplishment and value of such painters as Edward Hopper, Balthus, and Christian Bérard, to make "a random list," but "they do not belong to the history of the style of painting that is specifically modern." He regrets that he has had to exclude, among others, Rivera, Orozco, Siqueiros, Pascin, Utrillo.

To me, such a history is unthinkable both in title and in scope. I would suggest titles for a history that would encompass the many trends in painting today: *A History of Contemporary Painting*, *A History of Painting of the Last Fifty Years*, or *A History of Painting of Our Time*.

Therefore, I would have preferred this symposium to be called "The Alienation of the Artist of Today."

As I mentioned before, artists have always been alienated in one way or another. Now I shall try to explain my theory concerning the double alienation of the contemporary artist. To put it briefly, pessimistic as it may sound, he is simply not *needed* in our society. His art or craft is not fulfilling a *needed* function for society anymore. The function of painting has been taken over by other media.

When I say that art has lost its function, I mean that our society no longer calls upon the artist to paint man's image, to depict historical events, to record the life of his time. For example: when the coronation of Napoleon took place, David was asked to paint the event, and the result is the magnificent canvas in the Louvre. He also recorded the death of Marat. Today, photography, movies and television graphically record the assassination of Kennedy, the visit of the Pope, the destruction in Vietnam; the skill and depth of the artist are no longer required for this. What is left for the artist to do?

He paints abstractly, non-objectively, contentlessly, kidding himself that he somehow mirrors and expresses his time. For that, skill is not required, ability to draw is not required. The visible world is no longer a subject for the painter. Such work has no intrinsic merit and therefore needs much rationalization and speculation to bolster it. But as you are aware, in spite of all the apologia and the sophistry on its behalf, the art just described is rapidly becoming passé, making way for other isms that follow one another in rapid and restless succession, pop art, op art, kinetic art, etc.—verily, the work of the artist who is doubly alienated.

Now for the subtitle: "Must the Artist Communicate with his Public?"—isn't that contradictory? There is an audience, which implies there is somebody to communicate with. If the artist claims it is unnecessary to communicate, then why exhibit? The important question is whether there is anything communicable in the profusion of work that is being shown in innumerable galleries and museums. In my opinion, there is not. Certainly there is an audience that visits exhibitions of such art, talks about it, and even buys it. I must say that, present company excluded, the audience of the subtitle is the most permissive, passive, and gullible that ever was.

September 26, 1966

Young artists in the initial stages of their career should be helped professionally by older, or recognized artists. I was. Today, however, young people have more opportunities and outlets for exhibiting their work and attracting a following. When I began to exhibit, New York City was virtually an artistic desert. There were only a dozen or so galleries. There was no Museum of Modern Art, no Guggenheim Museum, and the Whitney Museum was in its embryonic stage and was known as the Whitney Studio Club. In a sense, life was simpler for a young artist, less confusing. When his work somehow became noticed, he would be introduced to the Whitney Club, which was then the main gateway to an art career.

Though I began to exhibit comparatively late, I was fortunate. My first pictures, shown in a group exhibition, attracted the attention of the brilliant, young and already established painter, Alexander Brook. He sold one of them for me, and brought me into the Whitney Club. Thereafter, whenever I finished a painting in my spare time (I still had to do other work for a living), I would take it to the Club. Mrs. Force, the director, would emerge from her office, usually flanked by the two young artist aides (Carl Free and Edmund Archer), and ask: "How much do you want for this, Mr. Soyer?" I would mumble, "One hundred dollars," and she would pay it. One day, for a very detailed painting upon which I had worked many weekends, I asked for $200 and she gave it to me without hesitation. I went home and told my mother that now I felt like a real artist, people were paying good money for my pictures.

September 27, 1966

The famous 1929 crash did not affect me or my parents or anyone else I knew. We were poor and had nothing to lose. True, the Daniel Gallery soon folded up and was never able to make a comeback. I took four of my pictures and showed them around to other galleries. They all wanted to keep them on consignment, but because I needed money I wouldn't leave them on that basis. Finally, when I brought them to the Valentine Gallery, the owner paid me $500 there and then for the four of them. To me that was a huge sum.

The Valentine Gallery exhibited mostly French art. There I saw at close range paintings by Picasso, Soutine, Modigliani, occasionally even a Degas, a

Monet and other Impressionists. I was allowed to pull these paintings out of the racks in the back room and examine them closely. Only a few American painters were shown there: besides myself, there were Eilshemius, Milton Avery, the American primitive John Kane, and that strange personality, Myron Lechay, who was a deep and interesting painter of semi-abstract still-lifes, interiors and street scenes quite ahead of his time. Lechay is completely unknown today, one of the many unnoticed figures in American art. I remained with Valentine for several years and had three shows there.

Then about 1936 I left Valentine Dudensing, much to his chagrin, and joined the Associated American Artists, the precursor of all the lush galleries to come. Its director was the first to commercialize the fine arts on a big scale, but he finally strangled the gallery, and some of his artists too, with his entrepreneurship and excess zeal. I was enticed into joining this group by the charming and sincere Pegeen Sullivan, who herself left the gallery when it deteriorated into too much of a business venture. She came to my studio at 3 East 14th Street and assured me of the success and prestige of this gallery, pointing out that the three pillars of American painting of this period, Benton, Curry and Wood, had agreed to join. A more persuasive argument was a promise to see to it that I need no longer worry about my studio rent. In those days it was hard to maintain a studio.

September 29, 1966

The last time that Avrohom and Beyla came together to see an exhibition of mine was in 1933. Among the canvases was their double portrait painted a year before, somewhere in the Bronx. It shows them, not too old, but frail, in an atmosphere of melancholy foreboding, for my mother was already showing signs of her breakdown. It is emphatically not, as one of our "wise men" of art, Harold Rosenberg, expounded in a radio broadcast some time ago, when he cited this particular painting "by one of the Soyers" as a possible example of

69

"Jewish art," a picture of an elderly couple sitting at ease after a Sabbath meal. Nothing was farther from my mind; I painted this under the spell of Degas' "Absinthe Drinkers," and my aim was to convey not a Sabbath atmosphere but a mood of everydayness, like the gray mood in the Degas painting.

I did one more portrait of Avrohom, sitting alone against the background of his books. He was now frail, gentle, well-groomed and lonely. Even his two daughters, with whom he lived at times and who understood him more and were sensitive to his needs, were unable to create a real home for him now that Beyla was away. After his death we knew that he had found for himself a substitute satisfaction in the close, personal relationship with his students. He no longer had to struggle with unruly children; for some years now he had been teaching Hebrew literature at Yeshiva College and found a response and attention there which he no longer had with us.

We occasionally meet some of his former students, now in various professions. They tell us that he was more than an academic instructor, that he was their friend. They describe his warmth, devotion, imagination and sense of humor.

Avrohom died in 1940. I quote a line from his favorite Hebrew poet, Bialik: "*Hayah ish, v'ainenoo*"—"There was a man, and is no more."

I did not attend Avrohom's funeral; it was my turn to visit Beyla. I tried to tell her that Avrohom had died, but could not reach her. Her eyes were lustreless, as if without irises.

September 30, 1966
==

So many books are now being written about the 1930's. Fascism was then an established institution, and Nazism was gaining impetus. In our country, the long suppression of the Negroes was brought into focus by the Scottsboro case. Intellectuals were following with great interest what was going on in Russia, the first socialist state, and in 1936 the Spanish Civil War began.

Nicolaï Cikovsky

I was made aware of the importance of these events, first by Nicolaï Cikovsky, and later by my wife. Nick and I met in the Daniel Gallery. He had already experienced the upheavals in his native Russia. Naïve as I was then, he represented to me sophistication in art and life and political outlook. He was gay, exuberant, and romantic. A strong bond was soon formed between us by the Russian language. He often sang Russian folk songs, accompanying himself on a mandolin. He came to this country already an accomplished painter, having passed through all the isms that were prevalent in the early decades of this century in Russia—Cézanne-ism, cubism, constructivism, futurism. By the time I met him, Cikovsky was enamored with the art of Matisse. His work was colorful, gay, animated. It has remained so throughout the years.

It was Cikovsky who introduced me to the John Reed Club of Artists and Writers, which was organized about this time. I went to my first meeting, taking along the girl who had been posing for me that afternoon. She was hanging around my studio as I was getting ready to leave and so I invited her to come along.

We came into a large, bare room, the walls of which were covered with American and foreign posters against Fascism and war. At a long, makeshift table sat a group of men, among them Nicolaï Cikovsky, Bill Gropper, Adolph Wolf, Walter Quirt, Nemo Piccoli. I remember them so accurately because I made several sketches of them that evening, for in those days I sketched wherever I found myself. They stared amusedly and questioningly at me and the girl. After fidgeting self-consciously and realizing she was not expected, she said, "I'll see you tomorrow," and left.

The Club grew and expanded rapidly, with branches in several foreign countries. To me personally, the Club was of great significance, for it helped me to acquire a progressive world outlook, but I did not let it influence my art. My work never became politically slanted. I always painted only what I knew and saw around me. In the 1930's I painted many pictures of unemployed and homeless men, because I saw them everywhere. I did not paint so-called class-conscious pictures—flattering figures of workers, or overfed capitalists. But two of my paintings were done under the direct influence of the John Reed Club.

À Watteau

John and Alice Rewald

John Reed Club Meeting

One was of a girl making a speech to a group of demonstrators; later, inspired also by the resistance of the Spanish people to Fascism, I painted "Workers Armed."

Some of the artists who are well-known today were members of the John Reed Club. We held exhibitions in the clubrooms; we painted collective pictures satirizing the state of affairs and sent them to national exhibitions, signed "John Reed Club." Often the original sketches for these were made by Bill Gropper, known for his political cartoons. They attracted attention.

Important artists and writers who were not members of the Club were invited to speak. Once Heywood Broun came, big, sloppy lovable. Humorously, he told us how he once timidly picked up a *Daily Worker* and after cautiously

Sketch of Gropper at work by Raphael Soyer 1941

William Gropper

looking around him began to read it and became engrossed in its sports page, completely forgetting that it was a non-kosher, Communist paper. A slight, young woman came and fascinated us with her account of how she wrote *I Went to Pit College*. I don't at this moment recall her name. Lewis Mumford lectured on Orozco and showed slides of his work. Both the talk and the slides were enlightening. It was my first serious acquaintance with the work of this Mexican draftsman and mural painter, and I still recall vividly one slide of a gigantic Christ chopping up his own cross.

Once I came to a meeting late and heard a familiar-looking young man talk about art. After the lecture he greeted me and I recognized Meyer Schapiro, a former classmate of mine at the National Academy. He was then becoming known as an art historian and teacher. One of his statements has remained with me. I don't recall in what context he made it, but it was probably in criticism of the Club's philosophy of social realism—"No *Kapital* on art has yet been written," he said. Ironically, he, and others were soon to formulate an art dogma of their own, preaching the "truth" of non-objectivism and claiming it was *the* valid art of our times.

Mexican art was then very popular, and the members of the John Reed Club painted murals under the influence of Rivera, Orozco and Siqueiros, depicting the imprisoned Tom Mooney, the Scottsboro boys and marchers with placards demanding their freedom. Like Rivera, we included likenesses of one another and self-portraits in these pictures. I remember posing for a young painter, Hideo Noda, who put me in a Rivera-esque mural.

One memorable evening Rivera spoke at the Club. A noisy attack on him was made by some of the leading members for his deviations from orthodox Marxism. I watched with fascination this immovable, gigantic man towering above his obstreperous attackers, and I sketched him in his blue shirt and red tie.

Siqueiros was also in New York about that time. He organized a workshop where young artists painted under his direction, making posters for the Communist Party election campaign—huge portraits of Browder, Foster and others. For my taste, Siqueiros was too flamboyant, loud and didactic.

I liked Rivera more; I was spellbound by him.

Diego Rivera

The Museum of Modern Art put on an exhibition of Rivera's work. Shortly thereafter he painted the Rockefeller Center mural, which was later destroyed by his wealthy patron because Lenin and Trotzky were in it. This act of vandalism created great consternation among us artists, and we demonstrated outside the center with placards of protest.

Rivera continued to work here. Without remuneration he painted a series of murals depicting the history of social struggle in America from a Marxist point of view. He worked long hours at the New Workers School, somewhere on 14th Street. In the evening I would come to watch him and make sketches of this fat, patient, industrious artist as he worked on his huge, complex compositions with what seemed to me tiny brushes. Once I was introduced to him and we conversed briefly in Russian. Characteristically, I didn't pursue the acquaintance.

The Club established its own art school in which I was invited to teach. Completely unprepared, I timidly embarked upon my prolonged "extra-curricular" career as a teacher. We had many talented, enthusiastic and socially

76

aware young students. One has remained particularly vivid in my memory, a dark, sinuous girl with aggressive and questioning eyes, Ruth Gikow, now one of our recognized painters. A show of her work was held in the School and I wrote an introduction to it. Even then, she painted ordinary people in their daily environment, a subject matter not different from the picture of hers I saw several years ago in a large exhibition of American art in Paris.

I hope that someday a serious history will be written of the John Reed Club: how it came into being, what forces gave it energy and what influence it had upon the painting and writing of that time; the prime movers, among them—I came in contact mainly with the artists—William Gropper, Anton Refrigier, Louis Lozowick, Henry Glintenkampf (affectionately called "Glint"), Nicolaï Cikovsky, Walter Quirt (known as "Shorty"), and Phil Bard. Young Joe Jones, full of promise and enthusiasm, came from the Middle West and joined the Club. What a fascinating account it would be!

Jones, Glint, Phil Bard and "Shorty" Quirt are now dead. Phil was the youngest and one of the brightest of the group. He died only a few months ago. He came to pose for me not too long before he died, gaunt, bearded, dishevelled and poorly dressed. In spite of his physical handicaps, he kept all his sitting appointments. We talked about art, literature, politics. He even made a few sketches of me with his left hand during rest intervals.

The following is what I wrote for Phil's posthumous show.

I became acquainted with Phil Bard when I joined the stimulating group of artists and writers known as the John Reed Club, in the early thirties. Most of us were quite young then, but one of the youngest was Phil, a charming fellow, talented in several fields, knowledgeable, even sophisticated for his years. What struck me most even then, was his optimism in the face of adverse situations that arose in those turbulent years. This courageous attitude, which manifested itself in his leadership of the Artists' Union and in his activity in Spain with the Lincoln Brigade, served him well in later years in his own personal life, when his ravaging illness left him half-paralyzed. With indomitable will he trained himself to draw with his left hand and was able to be active artistically till the very end.

These drawings are at once strong and sensitive, searching, expressionistic. There is an accuracy about them, an incisiveness, that belie the difficulty he must have had to overcome in making them. They are drawn mostly with India ink and sharp pen, giving them

Phil Bard

the appearance of etchings scratched into hard, resisting material. Each drawing is well-composed, self-contained. They are mainly of people, of men, women, children—an all-absorbing interest he had consistently all through his life.

The John Reed Club remains most vividly in my memory, probably because it was my first participation as an artist in activities with other artists. It offered me an outlet from my own self-involvement.

One of the most important events in the thirties was the meeting of the "American Artists Congress Against War and Fascism," which united artists of all esthetic persuasions throughout the country. Stuart Davis was the national executive secretary, and the National Committee included such names as Lewis Mumford, Kuniyoshi, Weber, Gropper, George Biddle, Moses Soyer, Rockwell Kent, Peter Blume, Paul Manship, Karl Knaths, Margaret Bourke-White, Louis Lozowick and Niles Spencer. I quote from the introduction of the book *American Artists Congress 1936*, which recorded its proceedings:

> This was a meeting of 400 leading American artists, academicians and modernists, purists and social realists, who were brought together on a platform in defense of their common interests. . . .
>
> The purpose of this organization is to achieve unity of action among artists of recognized standing in their profession on all issues which concern their economic and cultural security and freedom, and to fight war, Fascism and reaction, destroyers of art and culture.

How valid these words, "war, Fascism, reaction, destroyers of art and culture," still are today, more than thirty years later! It is difficult to describe how deeply artists were affected by the events of the thirties, the anxieties, the struggle. Some artists were involved even to the extent of joining the Lincoln Brigade in support of the Loyalists in the Spanish Civil War, and gave their lives for what they believed to be the cause of world freedom. My natural low-pulsed reaction was influenced to the extent of painting a canvas which I called "Workers Armed" to describe the people's army against Fascism.

Almost twenty years later I once more became actively involved in a project with artists. I initiated the publication of *Reality—A Journal of Artists' Opinion*

Workers Armed

(1953, '54, '55). Looking back, it amuses me to think how long it took for us artists to come together, to get to know one another, to air our views on art and events, and finally to produce, once a year, those three slim issues of *Reality*. Our purpose was to discuss the changing and confusing art situation of the moment, to try to understand the abrupt ascendancy of abstraction and non-representationalism and their wholehearted promulgation by museums, art dealers and critics.

80

In the first issue of *Reality*, Henry Varnum Poor tells charmingly "How This Group Began":

The first meeting of this Group was in response to a postcard from Raphael Soyer in March 1950. About ten of us met at the Del Pezzo Restaurant in New York. I recall Kuniyoshi, Sol Wilson, Raphael Soyer, Edward Hopper, Ben Shahn, Leon Kroll, Joseph Hirsch, and Philip Evergood.

We found it very pleasant to sit around a table and talk about what we believed in as painters, and of what we found wrong with the world. We felt that regardless of what might grow out of this, the meeting was worthwhile in just bringing us together, as otherwise we had very little communication with each other. So we met again, and the group kept growing.

From the wide diversity of the work and points of view represented, it was obvious this would never be a close-knit group like "The Eight" in America, or the French Impressionists who were working with very closely related ideas. We have tried to state our common beliefs, make some sort of Credo, but without complete success. I was for simply saying that we believed in, and loved the "Object," the "Image." That we were all objective painters, and so, conversely, we thought non-objective painting was a blind alley. But we found that what we were most "against" was not any way of painting, but the forces in our art world that threw things out of balance. Museums and critics were so quick to surrender all the values that we felt were permanent, and thus were making of our profession a thing of cults and fads, and obscurity and snobbery.

So, like the liberals in a free society, it is easier to state what we are against than what we are for. We are for the maintenance of values and liberties that we already have. To restate them means reviewing the whole history of art, or making generalizations that seem like clichés. We are against all forces that set up false values, that substitute obscurity for clarity, and that imperil our democracy.

So, here in this journal we make our statement. Whether we shall have a name, whether we shall form an organization, is all in the future. Now we are just "Artists."

It was not until three years after this first meeting that *Reality* made its appearance with a statement signed by forty-six artists. Here is an excerpt from that statement:

All art is an expression of human experience. All the possibilities of art must be explored to broaden this expression. We nevertheless believe that texture and accident, color, design, and all the other elements of painting, are only the means to a larger end, which is the depiction of man and his world.

Today, mere textural novelty is being presented by a dominant group of museum officials, dealers, and publicity men as the unique manifestation of the artistic intuition. This arbitrary exploitation of a single phase of painting encourages a contempt for the taste and intelligence of the public. We are asked to believe that art is for the future, that only an inner circle is capable of judging contemporary painting, that everybody else must take it on faith. These theories are fixed in a ritual jargon equally incomprehensible to artist and layman. This jargon is particularly confusing to young artists, many of whom are led to accept the excitation of texture and color as the true end of art, even to equate disorder with creation. The dogmatic repetition of these views has produced in the whole world of art an atmosphere of irresponsibility, snobbery, and ignorance.

The first issue of *Reality* also contained a letter to the Museum of Modern Art requesting that "non-abstract forms of art be given the same serious and scholarly consideration that the Museum has extended to abstract art recently," and that a conference be called "to help resolve some of the problems involved." Such conferences were later held, but the directors denied they were giving undue attention to non-objectivism.

We did not foresee the furious reaction our little publication would arouse on the part of the Museum of Modern Art, the critics, and other art publications. The Museum sent a letter by messenger to the members of our editorial board in which was implicit a warning against Communist influences. *Art News* stooped low enough to editorialize: "We prefer not to do a Voltaire to defend our attackers from the McCarthys or Donderos if and when the moment to do so arrives." In reply, in the second issue of *Reality*, we expressed our disappointment "in our enemies—we would expect issue to be taken with us on a higher level than proved to be the case."

I realize now that such hysterical reactions were inevitable in those McCarthy days. At the same time, however, we received ridiculous letters from some lunatic organizations wanting "to join in the war against the ungodly Communists of the Museum of Modern Art and the *Art News*"!

Art Digest, for its part, accused the signers of our statement of purely materialistic motives—fear of loss of prestige and income as artists and art teachers. Looking through my old papers I found a letter I wrote to the editors of the *Art Digest* answering this charge and others:

To the Editor:

Now that the hue and cry is almost over, and the editorials and "open letters" have been written (only a part of one more issue of *Art Digest* is to be devoted to a symposium on *Reality*, with statements by several "seceders"), I would like to express some personal thoughts not only as a "reactionary totalitarian" signer of the now celebrated statement in *Reality*, but also as a reader of *Art Digest*. It is interesting and significant that these "seceders" bolted only *after* the Modern Museum's open letter and all other editorials in the art magazines were printed. One can make of that what one will.

I am writing this on my own, I have not contacted anyone else on the editorial board since they are all scattered for the summer. I am amazed at the personal attacks in the magazines. I am amazed that such a civilized publication as *Reality* should arouse such violent, personal diatribes. One editor hysterically threatened this group of distinguished artists with a "McCarthy" treatment!

Your magazine goes as far as hinting that most of the signers, "veterans in art," have an ulterior motive, to regain what you call their low prestige in teaching, which means a loss of pupils, and, therefore, of financial security. May I urge the editors not to worry about the prestige of these distinguished painters—it is as secure as ever. To follow your own line of thought, is it possible that the existing art magazines are fearful of competition from another art publication? Seriously, nothing like that entered into the planning of *Reality*, it is not a business venture. Isn't it possible to take at face value the thought expressed in *Reality*, that a group of artists of high achievement, without regard for their own financial status, were really concerned about the state of art in our country in our time?

Now, you may be interested to know that the response to *Reality* was overwhelming, both in number as well as in positive approval. We had to make a second printing of the first issue, the demand has been so great that even a third edition could easily be used. We have had some wonderfully intelligent letters from art students, teachers and museum directors all over the country, as well as from the lay public, lovers of art. You must be conscious of the impact *Reality* has had upon the art world, witness your own columns of open letters which, by the way, are not *all* antagonistic to the challenge of *Reality*. You yourself, in answer to one letter, agree that "it is high time for some plain talk." . . . In the July 19th issue of the *New York Times*, Howard DeVree, in an interesting article evaluating the accomplishments of the various non-objective movements in art, seems to be doubtful of the permanence of their contribution to American art. I was glad to see that he deplores the negative attitude of young artists to the importance of good drawing and knowledge of tradition. Am I presumptuous in thinking that this article may be a result of the appearance of *Reality*?

These are indeed trying and confusing times. We have been called every name in the book, but has that ever deterred any forward-looking person from acting according to his honest convictions? What you call the "language of reaction" may really be the most advanced thoughts of these times.

From this letter one may get a fair idea of the reaction to *Reality*—the hostility on one side and the enthusiastic reception on the other. Needless to say, the letter was never printed, but neither was the announced symposium of the "seceders."

I learned much about the people with whom I worked on this venture. Some of those who replied most eagerly to my first call became the "seceders" the moment we were attacked, but others were steadfast. Henry Varnum Poor, from whom I got the most pessimistic response, became the prime mover and leading editorial writer once he joined.

As I look through the issues of *Reality* now, I am fascinated by such articles as "Fads and Academies," by Isabel Bishop; "Man is the Center," by Jack Levine; "Humanism in Art," by Honoré Sharrer; Hopper's personal credo; a letter to Huntington Hartford by George Biddle; letters from Paris by Guy Pène du Bois; letters from the Europeans Henry Moore, Bernard Berenson, Guttuso, Matta, Kokoschka, Marcel Gimond; three articles by Maurice Grosser devastatingly exposing the naïve zeal and the ridiculous jargon of the early apologists for non-objectivism. I find myself still moved by the eloquent letters we printed from readers all over the world, both artists and laymen, expressing their concern for the state of art.

Why did this magazine cease to exist after only three issues? Simply because we'd had our say, we could not go on repeating ourselves, and there was no one among us who could expand what we had already said into further articles.

All the material for *Reality* was sent to my studio. I kept it for some years and then sent part of it to the Archives of American Art in Detroit and the rest to Cornell University.

Henry Varnum Poor

In April 1935, after one of my early one-man shows at the Valentine Gallery, of which my share of the sales was $1,050, I went off by myself to Europe on the old *Ile de France*. It was a cold, miserable and rocky sailing, and it was cold for a long time after I reached Paris. In the morning I would rush from my room on Rue Vavin to the Dome for coffee, and sit as long as possible near the pot-bellied stove. It was my first trip to Europe since my father brought our family over to America.

I was completely disenchanted with everything. I didn't have enough money, or friends, and I didn't know the language. Paris was bleak. Artists were standing on line for soup at the government kitchens. Those sitting in the Montparnasse cafés, and they seemed to be there all day long, were mainly from the Eastern European countries, not accepted by the native artists, yet snubbing the few Americans who were there for just a short time. They had been sitting stranded in these cafés for many years, and kidded themselves into believing they were Parisians.

Even the museums in Paris disappointed me. They had not yet been renovated, and the walls were heavy with dark, opaque, badly lit paintings.

From Paris I went to London. I was cold there too. My stay coincided with the Silver Jubilee celebration of King George V, and Buckingham Palace was besieged by the populace waiting for a glimpse of the royal family who would appear on the balcony from time to time. People came from all over the country, poorly dressed, and they clung to the gates of the Palace like something out of Dickens, men, women and children shivering with cold, their bad teeth chattering.

Even the huge British Museum depressed me strangely. Cold and dank, it seemed to me a graveyard of past civilizations.

Neither in London, nor later in Russia, did knowledge of the language help to dispel my feelings of disenchantment, loneliness and irritability. Only when Rebecca joined me on my return to Paris did I feel relieved. Not for another quarter of a century were we able to go to Europe again.

October 3, 1966

In a London bookshop I picked up a slim volume of poetry containing selections from Gregory Corso, Lawrence Ferlinghetti and Allen Ginsberg, and I've been reading it on the boat going home. I wonder how they are judged by the more universally accepted poets, how they measure up in their ability to express and convey feelings, in their technique and imagery.

I know little about poetry, but I am moved by the plainness of Gregory Corso's "Marriage," "Man," and "Writ on the Eve of My 32nd Birthday"; by Ferlinghetti's "In Goya's Greatest Scenes," and by his evocative poem to Allen Ginsberg entitled "He." I regret that his "Autobiography" ends so soon; I could read on and on. Allen Ginsberg's outpourings in "Europe Europe," "America" and "Magic Psalm" encompass much of our time and our world. I like these compassionate blasphemous, hallucinatory poems; these poets, in truth, reveal themselves.

I once said to Allen Ginsberg, "Your style, the way you talk to yourself in your poems, and the way you mention your friends, Kerouac, Burroughs by name reminds me of Walt Whitman, or Mayakovsky, or Yessenin. But their poetry, even the melancholy Yessenin's, is so affirmative compared to yours. You know Mayakovsky's poem about the sun coming in to have tea with him. How full of life, how energetic it is! But you begin, 'You are rotting, Allen Ginsberg,' and you go on to describe your deterioration. I smell death, decaying flesh, when I read your poems."

"What's wrong with that?" Ginsberg answered. "I traveled in India, all over, not just where the tourists go. They don't bury their dead as we do, they burn them. Not in crematoria, but in the open. These funeral fires never cease.

I saw burning corpses, I saw what happens to flesh, skin, eyes. People pass by these fires, children pass them by, without so much as looking at them. It's normal—death, mortality, decay of flesh are real, like life. Why not write about them?"

Is this kind of poetry analogous to avant-garde painting which also claims to mirror our confused, unhappy times? If so, the poetry makes more sense to me. Perhaps through the medium of words it is more possible to do what the avant-garde painters say they are doing with their various abstractions. For what meaning is there in imageless blobs of color on a canvas?

July 6, 1967

It's been months since I wrote in this journal. My exhibition is drawing near. This morning, before leaving for Vinalhaven, I was with Lloyd Goodrich, who came to discuss the material for the catalog (he calls it "the Book") for my retrospective exhibition due to open October 24th. Later, at Goodrich's request, we went to my studio where I showed him my unfinished composition, "A Watteau," which he praised, to my delight. This is a picture of what can often be seen these days in Central Park, groups of friendly young people playing musical instruments, beating drums, clapping out rhythms with their hands, sticks or with any other kind of object. The central figure is a girl with a rapt expression holding a daffodil in one hand, the other raised, open-palmed. She is symbolic, if you will, of peace, youth, goodwill, friendship.

I call the picture "A Watteau" because the scenes in Central Park bring to mind the paintings of Watteau: musical parties of men and women in parks. As a matter of fact, I based this composition on his large, well-known painting of the single, white-clad Pierrot on a hill with musicians below.

Quite a few of my pictures of contemporary life are inspired, either in spirit or in composition, by some classical painting.

David and Marusia Burliuk

Vinalhaven

Vinalhaven—July 12, 1967

It is so foggy that I decided to work on this journal instead of painting outdoors. We're in Vinalhaven after an absence of two years. The only perceptible change is that the neighboring children are bigger. As always upon our arrival, they came to greet us with their innocent frankness.

The landscape hasn't changed much, but here an old, unused pier finally crumbled and collapsed into the bay, and there the roof of an abandoned house has become less visible because the trees around it have grown. The major changes are on Main Street—the A & P burned to the ground in what must have been a spectacular fire in the middle of the night. Opposite this gap, at the entrance to the parking lot, now stands a traditional American eagle, one of the two salvaged from the demolished Penn Station in New York.

"The other eagle was made from Vinalhaven granite," we were told by a local housewife, "but for some reason we got this one."

Set up astride two slabs of native granite, this ghastly bird does not enhance Main Street, esthetically or otherwise.

The pace on this island is unusually slow this summer. There's less activity, fewer summer people, less traffic, making its insularity poignantly apparent. On the eve of my retrospective exhibition, this remoteness is conducive to rumination and introspection. I find myself constantly mulling over the procedures of my art life.

In my mind I see my paintings on the walls of the Whitney Museum, from the earliest to "A Watteau" (I hope to finish it when I come back to New York). The first nude—which I painted independently after leaving art school —stands white against a red background, naked, chaste, with clasped hands. Then "Portrait of the Artist's Mother"—an immigrant woman sitting on a carved chair against a flower-papered wall, one hand on her abdomen as in Raphael's "La Bella Gravida" in the Pitti Palace, the other hand, with the wedding ring on her finger, listlessly hanging over the arm of the chair. She is heavy and melancholy; the yellowish lace of her red dress is like a golden chain in a Renaissance portrait.

"Portrait of the Artist's Father"—a head cut out from an ambitious composition which, lacking skill, I was not able to consummate then. Crude, with an implausible combination of overtones from Van Gogh and Rembrandt.

"The Bridge"—technically almost a beginner's work, but with the poetic naïveté of Rousseau's vision. I have never surpassed these early pictures.

How extraordinary is an artist when he is young! What a confusion of visions, emotions, perceptions, hopes and plans embroils him! He is young and old at the same time, simple and instinctively wise.

It has always been my contention that with rare exceptions artists do not become deeper or greater with the years. They change, to be sure, they acquire technical skill and become complex and rich in color. With years of painting, however, it becomes increasingly difficult to hold on to the indefinable freshness of youthful vision and to spontaneous reaction. How often are the early, simple, self-contained canvases of well-known artists preferable to their later ambitious, flamboyant ones.

I'm amazed by the longevity of my early paintings. Hanging on walls, hidden in closets by relatives and friends, covered with dust, at times amateurishly cleaned or oversprayed with varnishes, they were preserved and eventually restored.

This fantasy about my forthcoming show was interrupted by my wife's exclamation, "Marusia Burliuk died!" She showed me the *New York Times* with the obituary notice.

How soon Maria Nikiforovna followed her husband, David Burliuk, who died six months ago. There is a famous story by Gogol, "Old-Time Landowners," in which a husband and wife are described as so inseparably attached to each other that when one dies, the other follows shortly after. This is exactly what happened with the Burliuks; the devoted wife and companion of many years who was ever at his side while he was painting, writing, reminiscing, could not live without her husband. She was the curator, archivist and editor of his books, paintings and documents. She published "Color and Rhyme" for many

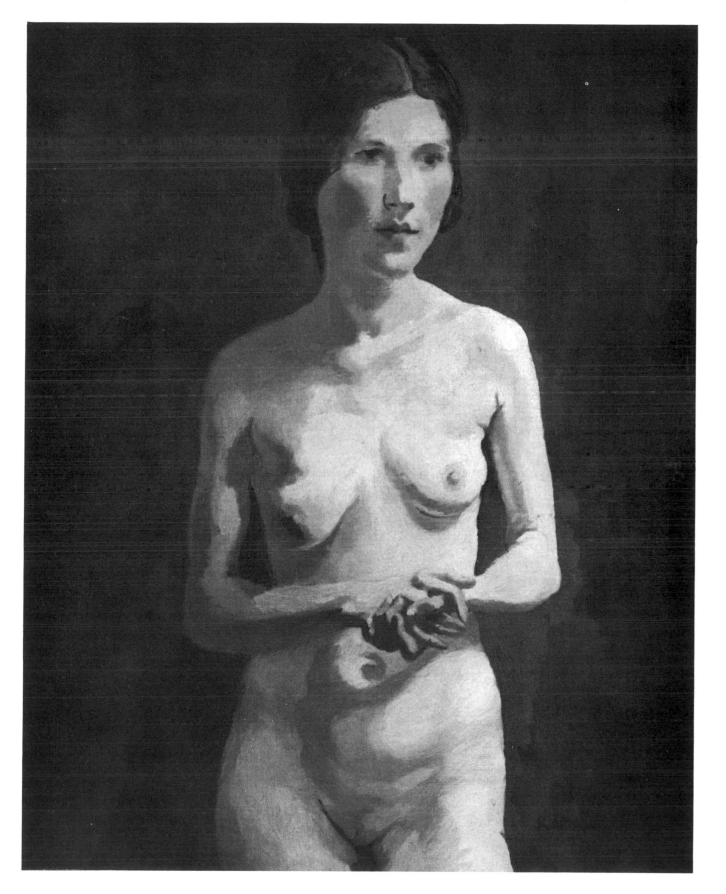

First Nude

The Bridge

years, a strange conglomeration of memoirs, notes, letters, reproductions, poems and newspaper clippings of everything pertaining to the life and work of David Burliuk and to all those who touched his life. This unique publication, half English and half Russian, was printed at their own expense and sent gratis to their friends all over the world.

Marusia Burliuk was unforgettable in her long, wide skirt, ruffled blouse, a small hat perched on her disheveled hair, her flushed face enlivened by wide-open, inquisitive eyes—like a character out of a Russian play.

Only three months ago I received this touching letter from Marusia Burliuk which I shall now translate as literally as I can.

Mrs. Burliuk's letter:

My dear and kind Rebecca and Raphael,

I am grateful to Raphael for the excellent article about Papa Burliuk. He is alive in it. I sent $8 to *Dialog* for 10 copies of the magazine with your article.

The 15th of April I signed a contract to publish "Color and Rhyme No. 63" in the Russian language, containing Burliuk's poems and my memoirs for the years 1936–39. This will be the end of my 37 years of publishing. This was the last wish of the living Burliuk: "Don't mourn. Live by yourself and finish up my work." These, literally, were his last words.

This week I'm staying with Jeannette, and I shall go to a specialist to find out about the pain in my chest which does not let me live or breathe. In the country the winds come from the ocean, the flowers are beginning to open up. In the home of Papa Burliuk there will never be any more living flowers. Neither he nor I need them any more. And in the garden, anyone who wants may pick them and carry them away. Burliuk never handled living flowers. He never touched earth. He was strangely allergic to it and it made him deathly sick. He almost died 5 times—in Russia twice, in Japan once, and in America twice. The last time his blood poisoning was checked by Dr. Rubler who came at midnight in 1950.

All the still-lifes he painted were set up by me, and if Burliuk didn't like them he would ask me to rearrange them. Burliuk worked with materials harmful to his health, and I would sit near him and rub his hands with a special lotion, not with soap and water, and his face, too. The fear of losing Burliuk was with me all my life. Our children did now know about this danger. These are a few lines about his hands and his face.

I thank Raphael again for the excellent article.

Greetings and love,

Marusia Burliuk, April 21

The article referred to in this letter follows:

David Burliuk died without knowing that he had been elected to the American Institute of Arts and Letters, the highest recognition for creative people in our country. How he would have revelled in this, for he was a great believer in honors, rewards, fame, immortality. I believe that history will catch up with this old "cubo-futurist," as he liked to call himself. He was, in his own words, the "father" of modernism in Russian art, one of the founders of *Die Blaue Reiter*, together with Kandinsky, Paul Klee and Franz Marc. In Russia, before the Revolution, he helped to organize international exhibitions of modern art in 1911–12, in which Matisse, Delaunay and Picasso participated.

In 1922 Burliuk came to the United States with other Russian artists. I still remember the mammoth exhibition of their work at the Brooklyn Museum, but after all the fanfare and the initial excitement of this show died down he was left neglected for many years. That was a barren period in American art. Even native artists found it hard to live by their painting.

But David Burliuk was indomitable, courageous and optimistic. He set himself to paint New York scenes: the East Side, the Bowery, the Bronx, and later the landscapes of Long Island, with the same gaiety and vigor with which, in Russia, he did "Ukraina," "Market Day," "Woman with Cow" and other themes. He remained profoundly Russian all his life in this country, often turning to his native land for subject matter: "Tea Drinkers," "Harvest," etc. I remember two variations of a particularly striking canvas, "Tolstoy and Lenin—Unconquerable Russia," in which Lenin and Tolstoy are shown plowing Russian soil, symbolizing the deep, great changes they caused in their country.

How hard it is for me to appraise fully the work of a man who lived 84 years and worked until the very end. I can only say how deeply I sense in Burliuk's art his one-ness with the visible world. I'm referring mainly to his work done in this country, which I know best. His landscapes of earth, water, flowers, sky are bursting with vitality, exuberance and elemental force. Scattered all over them are people, horses, cows, in many colors, without perspective, without logic. But strangely, the effect is one of joy and life.

One hot afternoon on Long Island, Nicolaï Cikovsky and I went with Burliuk to paint a landscape. I admired the energy with which he started to work, how he applied great brush-strokes of thick paint on the rough canvas—*tachisme*, action-painting, but transferring living nature on the raw, dead surface of the canvas. After a few hours Cikovsky and I began to pack up but Burliuk turned his easel around and started to paint the scene from another angle. There was still some light and he couldn't bear to tear himself away from his work. We watched him in the fading light. Once in a while he would gently brush a mosquito from his face.

Years ago Burliuk presented my wife and me with a self-portrait which still hangs in our house. He sits before an open book with a pen in his hand. On the table are a globe of the world, a glass of wine, bread and fruit, a manuscript, an old watch. In the background are shelves of books, paintings, a head of his wife by Noguchi; through the window one sees a landscape with a setting sun and a rising moon. At the bottom of the canvas is his inscription: "D. Burliuk, painter and poet."

After the funeral we went to visit his family. The house we knew so well, filled with books and paintings, seemed strangely empty without the bent figure of old Burliuk in his stocking-hat at his easel. There were his brushes still wet with paint; his palette covered with a white cloth after the day's work to keep the dust from the paint; an unfinished still-life on the easel.

July 15, 1967

I wonder how my street scenes, painted so long ago and generally unknown, will hold up. I did them out of doors when the streets of New York were still accessible, when perspective and space had not yet been completely devoured by traffic. Today "Corlears Hook Point," "Under the Bridge," "Water Street" seem strangely idyllic. I remember the lyrical mood I was in while painting them. I was enamored of space; it had a positive existence for me and played the major role in the composition. How unrecognizable New York has become!

Then appear (as I imagine them on the walls of the Museum) my brown paintings of the unemployed. The men in them are static, they just stand on street corners, and sit in parks, in missions, in relief stations. They don't reflect anger, not even frustration. I saw them all over, doing nothing. By temperament, probably, I chose to paint these silent, non-demanding figures rather than the demonstrations, clashes with police so often painted by some of my fellow artists during the Depression. Among the "transients" I painted my own face, yawning, perhaps to emphasize the debilitating boredom of their lives.

To compose these pictures I would make sketches in Union Square, Washington Square, Sixth Avenue or some corner of the Bowery or 14th Street. For the picture "Reading from Left to Right," I used a photograph by Ben Shahn of menus written with dissolved Bon Ami cleanser on a Bowery window.

Lloyd Goodrich told me that many of my portraits of artists will be shown at my retrospective. Some of them are studies from life for "Homage to Thomas Eakins"; others are the ones I painted in the early forties and exhibited under the title "My Contemporaries and Elders." I still regret that I painted them at a time when my work was at a low ebb.

I have observed that many of us pass through a critical period during our middle years, when our work often becomes pedestrian, dull, lethargic.

Fortunately, some of us become aware of this static state and are able to pull ourselves out of it.

Several times in recent years one or another of these old portraits have turned up under wrong titles: a portrait of Moses Soyer was considered my self-portrait; one of Mervin Jules was called a portrait of Jack Levine; the one of Ernest Fiene was thought to be Thomas Benton, whom I never painted. When these were brought to me for authentication I couldn't decide whether to be annoyed or amused.

A quarter of a century has gone by. I kept a diary while I painted these artists, but I destroyed it one moody morning. Now many of them are dead, but they still live on in my memory, for I studied their faces and their gestures intently.

Joseph Stella came to my studio at 1 Union Square and sat down heavily on a wooden folding chair, both hands resting on his cane. That's how I painted him, large and ceremonious. He spoke loudly in vivid, rhetorical language, interspersed with four-letter words to emphasize his contempt for some people and things. With great drama he described the triumphs and defeats of his career. It was hard to capture his face, especially his eyes, which were never steady, at times opening wide, and then almost disappearing in his big, flabby face. But he encouraged me with loud exclamations: "You're getting my girth, you're getting my girth!"

I visited Stella at his place on East 14th Street once when I was least expected (he had no phone). I can't forget that visit. He lived alone. I found him sitting at a table with his back to the door, eating minestrone from a deep bowl. To say he was informally dressed would be an understatement. He turned around quickly as I came in. His sparse hair was not combed flat as in my portrait, but was standing up, white, like a halo. "Excuse my attire," he said with dignified embarrassment. "You're an artist—you understand. I don't have to change. We're alone in the studio."

Stella showed me many pictures of different periods and styles, a variety of subject matter in many media: early skillful and delicate drawings in pencil and colored chalk; religious pictures; abstract studies for his Brooklyn Bridge

Reading from Left to Right

Joseph Stella

and Coney Island compositions. He spread out on the floor pastels of lush tropical plants and flowers. In the center of one of these flowers a living bedbug was crawling. At the other end of this unattractive room was a crude sink stacked with unwashed dishes.

I felt a deep sympathy for this aging artist in his dismal surroundings.

How different he looks from the way he sat formally in my studio, I thought to myself. This is how I should have painted him. Here, against these walls of greasy, sickly yellow.

Burliuk was in his vigorous sixties when he came to pose, tall and upright. He arranged everything himself: he put the small table in the middle of the room; and on a sheet of white paper he wrote in block letters with a red pencil two lines of one of his Russian post World War I poems:

VSIAKI MOLOD, MOLOD, MOLOD,
V ZHIVOTIEH TCHERTOVSKY GOLOD,

which means, "We are young, young, young, In our belly a devilish hunger."

(As I write this I am reminded of Henry Miller's constant hunger at about the same time, described in *The Tropic of Cancer*. He quotes Emerson as saying, "A man is what he thinks of all day," and exclaims, "If that is so, I'm a gut, a great big empty gut.")

"Paint me as a futurist poet," Burliuk said. He sat down very straight, and composed his face in the expression he wanted, like an actor. He held the red pencil in a pose of writing and remained still, seldom blinking his one good eye.

I painted John Sloan in his studio in the Chelsea Hotel. His diminutive wife, Dolly, was still alive and darted in and out. He wore a white shirt and held a pipe. His beautiful pompadour was deceptive, it was just one big band of hair which he ingeniously combed over his bald expanse. At that time he was occupied with copying in oil one of his well-known etchings of two women in a fashionable carriage. He stood very close to the canvas, scrutinizing both the etching and the oil, his bulging eye peering through the heavy lens of his glasses. I saw him sideways, in profile. He copied skillfully and easily.

John Sloan

One morning I found Sloan in low spirits. He said that the curator of the Tate Gallery had come to look at his work and seemed to prefer a few of his early canvases, ignoring all that he had done subsequently. "I did those things when I was quite young, in my spare time. I didn't even consider myself a painter then," he grumbled. "Everything I've done since doesn't seem to count."

I tried to comfort him by saying, "The curator likes your early pictures probably because they make him think of Sickert, whom he admires. There's no denying that Sickert is one of the best painters in England today."

Arshile Gorky was a "contemporary." I knew him better than my "elders," Weber, Sloan, Hartley. He liked to come to my studio, which was across from where he and Agnes lived on Union Square. He would appear several times a week and sketch whomever I happened to be painting. When the Burliuks posed for me, Gorky sat quietly to one side and diligently drew them. His Seurat-like profile of Burliuk hangs on my wall today. He made many drawings of me too, and I painted and drew him whenever I had a chance. He was a fascinating subject—tall, thin, with deer-like eyes, a naïve and haunted expression and blue-black hair. He had beautiful hands.

His clothes were like his paintings in color and texture, harmonious and esthetic: a brown corduroy jacket, a red scarf loose around his neck, its folds arranged with deliberate intent. How he kept it in place, even when he moved about, was a mystery. He loved soft, colorful stocking caps. His tweed overcoat hung on him, loose and long.

No one was more involved in art than Arshile, and not just in his own. He lived intimately with art. His taste was infallible. He could point out the salient elements in a Vermeer, a Degas, an Ingres. He usually had in his pocket a small Ingres monograph which he would open and study earnestly, standing up, his body rhythmically swaying, as though reading a prayer book. In these small black and white Ingres reproductions he pointed out to me shapes and patterns, how self-contained they were, dissociated from one another, but how, together, they formed a great compositional unit.

99

While I was painting Arshile's blue-black hair, he said to me, "Why do you make this shine in my hair? It breaks up its shape, and the pattern of the whole painting is spoiled." I removed the highlight, and to my surprise the picture improved. It was a small but important criticism.

I visited him very often, too. His large room on Union Square was like his art, like the clothes he wore, in impeccable taste. In one corner, against a gray wall, was a still-life on a table, almost a painting; one had no need to reproduce it on a canvas. No pictures were on the wall; they were all neatly stacked in the racks. The room was permeated with the warmth that emanated from his personality.

One late afternoon after a long conversation, Arshile impulsively took out two small paintings from the racks, a self-portrait and a head of his sister, Vartoosh, and gave them to me. When I offered him at a later date the portrait I did of Agnes pregnant with their first child, he refused it, even though Agnes was anxious to have it. Sullenly he muttered, "Don't give it to me. I don't collect. You have a romantic life with pictures. I may someday suddenly paint over it."

In those days it was common to scoff at Arshile. Artists and critics alike considered him characterless, derivative, imitative to a point of plagiarism. He defended himself against such accusations by saying that he had a right to imitate the masters from whom he could learn, like a child who learns from his parents by imitating them.

"Yes," he told me on several occasions, "Cézanne is my father, Picasso is my mother."

I always felt there was an element of his own in all of Gorky's paintings, a poetic, indefinable quality no matter which masters they recalled. The portrait of his mother and himself as a child—how he labored on that painting—is pure Gorky, though one can trace in it Cézanne, Picasso, and Gauguin, as well as Coptic and even icon art. I can never look at this painting without emotion—how much this awkward, shy Armenian boy resembles the man Gorky whom I knew. After seeing it at the Whitney Museum, I wrote him that it was one of the most beautiful paintings of its time. He was then recovering from a serious illness, and when I saw him later he told me how much that letter meant to him at that moment.

"One other artist wrote me a similar letter," he said, "Yves Tanguy."

It may be presumptuous of me, but I must express regret at the fact that Arshile did not paint more pictures like the "Artist and His Mother," "Vartoosh," "Myself and My Imaginary Wife," and his flower pieces. Most of the work produced in the last five years of his life was done after he came in contact with the Surrealists, André Breton, and others then in America. How naïvely flattered he was to be accepted by them! He was essentially unsure, without faith in himself, humble, though on the surface he could appear arrogant and contemptuous of the work of others.

"Make my eyes as blue as hell," Marsden Hartley instructed me emphatically in his quiet voice. Were I painting him today, I would follow his instruction, but I was then, alas, engrossed in naturalistic rendering, and lost emphasis of any kind in the process of many repaintings. His eyes were strikingly blue, and I should have painted them "blue as hell." As a matter of fact this portrait, the smaller one of two that I made of him, was never quite finished. Hartley interrupted it himself. He came one morning, opened up a little newspaper package to disclose two dental plates of upper and lower teeth. Deftly he set them in his mouth, pointed to the portrait and said, "Without the teeth my face was like a garbage can. Make a new one of me now, a big one."

Hartley was well-mannered, gentle and vain. There was a fresh red carnation in his coat lapel every day. He told me that once another artist stared at him for a long time, much to his discomfiture. "Why are you looking at me so long?" Hartley asked him. "When I go home I'll paint your portrait from memory," the other artist answered. "He did, and it was awful," Hartley continued. "I even dreamt about it. I was standing near a body of water and I saw this weird head washed ashore."

I painted him just before Hudson Walker began to draw him back into the public eye. Apparently he had been in an artistic eclipse. Once, while he was posing, there was a knock at the door, and Hartley, who by now felt at home in my studio (he even ate his sandwiches there, which he brought wrapped in a newspaper) opened the door. He bowed politely to a tall, good-looking girl and said, "How do you do. I am Marsden Hartley."

"Who?" the girl asked. "I never heard of you." Her rudeness was unusual and unintentional. "Is Mr. Soyer here?" When the girl left, Hartley turned to me and said, "How pleasant it is to be obscure." His gentle voice was tinged with bitterness, I thought.

I preferred the small portrait I did of Hartley, with the toothless mouth like a cut in his face, and that was the one I exhibited. Hartley never forgave me. I saw him a few years later at the Rosenberg Gallery where he had his last show. He died soon after. He was then flabby, sleepy-looking and slow moving. He put his limp hand into mine, looked at me in rebuke, and said in his peculiarly soft manner, "Why did you exhibit that toothless image of me?"

Vinalhaven—July 18, 1967

I started my independent painting in the mid-twenties at a time when the art of the Impressionists, the nudes of Renoir and Degas became fully accepted in this country. Until then the female nude was rarely found in American painting. The only great nudes were by Thomas Eakins in his portrayal of the sculptor Rush working in his studio. These I came to know belatedly. The nudes of Henri, Sloan and Bellows left me cold, had no effect on my work. It was Pascin who created a cult among the younger artists for painting and drawing the female figure nude and semi-clothed. His drawings and paintings which I saw first at the Daniel, Downtown and Weyhe Galleries, stimulated me to hire my first model.

Is it because paintings of women are generally more appealing than those of men that my pictures of them became better known? Before I realized it I began to be called a painter of girls. But the Whitney exhibition will show that I have often painted men with great attention.

My early pictures were self-portraits—drawings, etchings, lithographs and the first efforts in painting with oils. I would look at myself in the mirror and patiently try to copy my features. Even later, whenever I lacked subject matter I would paint myself. Seen together, these pictures record the passage of time.

In the fifties I painted in quick succession a number of small self-portraits all in the same pose, my face resting in the palm of my hand. Once, alone in the studio as I usually was when painting myself, I began to think of the self-portraits of some of my favorite artists, and it suddenly occurred to me to paint myself in this pensive pose alongside self-portraits of Rembrandt, Corot and Degas which I had copied from reproductions. Placing myself in their company was not a delusion of grandeur, but an expression of esteem and of love for their work.

Fifteen minutes before my exhibition opened to the public Rebecca and I were admitted to the Whitney. The first glance of rooms-opening-upon-rooms filled with my paintings was startling. It is hard to describe my feelings upon suddenly being confronted with so great a part of my lifework. I was engulfed in a panorama of canvases.

Looking at all these pictures I didn't know whether to be pleased or distressed by the sameness, the thread of continuity I found there. Though the men and women who people my canvases cover a span of forty years and more, they have changed little. Their costumes may differ slightly, but their bearing, their gestures, the atmosphere emanating from them, are hardly changed. There is the same detachment, the same dissociation even when grouped together, the same withdrawal, the same involvement with oneself. From the first to the last canvas there is no abrupt or sudden activity, no drama. On the whole, I was struck by a sense of the static, of repose. The gestures are restrained, the arms never too far away from the body. Even the walking figures and those engaged in work have an air of arrested motion. This is true even of my latest compositions ("Pedestrians," "Village East"). Like stills from some contemporary film; sitting, standing, walking, there is a feeling of waiting for some-

103

thing that is not even expected to come. Beckett's *Waiting for Godot* suddenly came to my mind.

All these paintings were done in New York, of its people, its streets, of myself, the members of my family, my friends. "Art is local," I said to myself, quoting from my favorite aphorism by Derain: "Stupidity is national, intelligence is international, art is local." I recalled the paintings I saw this morning at the Metropolitan Museum by Rembrandt, Degas, Eakins. "Art is local," I repeated to myself.

At the exhibition I particularly missed David and Marusia Burliuk. On one wall of the Whitney is a large conversation painting of artists, models and myself. Burliuk is pictured there, sitting venerably in the center. Another canvas shows him painting his patient wife. He would have been so pleased to see these, as if he himself were participating in the show. When I last saw him he complained softly, "Everything withers in me—my bones, my heart. Everything dries in me and shrinks."

Edward Hopper also looks down from these walls. In recent years I was flattered that he never failed to visit my one-man shows and always wrote me a curt note of praise. I missed him and his brief comments this time, for he died some months ago. He became so frail in the last two years of his life—after I painted him for "Homage to Thomas Eakins"—a huge, bent skeleton with skin like parchment.

Until about two years ago Rebecca and I would dutifully make a yearly visit to the Hoppers, climbing up the four steep flights to their home on Washington Square. Before each visit we had to phone several times, for Jo Hopper would invariably try to dissuade us from coming, either because "the house is in disorder," or because they had "not yet unpacked" from their return to New York even though it was months since their arrival from Cape Cod, or simply because "Eddie isn't up to it." Finally she would consent to our coming, and would receive us with her fussy cordiality, ushering us into her studio, a sunny room facing south. We always brought some memento—a little book on

Street Scene

Corlears Hook Point

Thomas Eakins, or some publication with a reference to Hopper.

In Jo Hopper's studio there was a permanent, never-changing exhibition of her paintings—pictures of her small, crammed world, of Truro, flower pieces, interiors of her room, and pictures of cats and pot-bellied stoves. Only once did we see Edward's studio, a large white-washed bare room with an etching press, an easel and nothing on the walls. Jo would daintily serve us bread-and-butter sandwiches and tea fragrant with a clove in each cup.

Once, years ago, we visited the Hoppers in their summer home perched by itself on one of the hills in Truro. Jo wrote us directions how to get to it and emphasized the difficulty of driving up the almost perpendicular road to the top. "Keep in the ruts," she warned. When we reached the house there was Hopper sitting in front of it looking out over the hills; we found Jo sitting in the back looking out over the ocean. "That's what we do all the time," she said sharply, "he sits in his spot and looks at the hills all day, and I look at the ocean, and when we meet there's controversy, controversy, controversy."

Their frugality amused us. When they took us out to dinner in Truro, it was not to any of the restaurants generally frequented by artists and their friends, but to "Bill's," a nondescript diner on the road. "The food here is better than in any of the high-tone places," Jo said with conviction.

Their house was stark and bare inside and outside, scrupulously clean and white. In a large room stood a huge easel which Hopper said he had made himself, pointing to a box in the corner containing the tools with which he made it. There was not a painting or even a bare canvas in sight. When I asked him what he was working on, he said, "I'm waiting for November when the shadows are longer and the landscape becomes more interesting, in fact, beautiful."

Frankly, a Hopper landscape has never enchanted me in the way a Corot or a Cézanne does. In spite of the universal acclaim for his work, I secretly find something lacking—intimacy, poetry, grace. I was never possessed by a desire to own a Hopper painting. But I liked him and admired him, and recognized his intelligence, integrity and non-conformity. In any exhibition of American paintings a Hopper stands out, uncouth, lonely and silent—like his house, like his easel, like himself.

Edward Hopper

Israel—May 25, 1968

A wit once said that Q.E.D. is put at the end of a proven theorem to tell a fool when to stop. At the risk of being called a fool I have decided to continue with my chronicle, for once again I am travelling, not painting, just looking at pictures in museums and galleries in foreign countries, with time often heavy on my hands.

Tel Aviv seethed with young people, for the most part dark-haired, suntanned, with high cheekbones and sensibly strong features. Their Hebrew is like a new language—guttural, strong, living, completely unlike the Hebrew I knew as a child, and without the accents and intonations of immigrants.

Ninety-nine percent of the tourists are Jews. They are pilgrims just as much as those who journey to Rome and Mecca, mostly unprepossessing middle-aged and elderly couples. (Age has always been unprepossessing to me.) In the fancy hotels the pilgrims are better dressed but otherwise the same, except that they seem to identify with Israel more arrogantly than the others, perhaps because they have investments there, or because they may have contributed money or time to Israeli causes.

We divided our two weeks between Tel Aviv and Jerusalem. All of Jerusalem was open to us. The Old City is like El Greco's Toledo: stony, hilly, yellowish white in glaring light. With half an ear I listened to the routine monologue of the guide, who pointed out the places of interest to the three religions. At the Wailing Wall we watched the praying of the devout—the men noisily chanting and swaying, separated from the women who were more reserved, standing silent, their faces pressed to the yellow stones of the ancient Wall.

It was the labyrinth of the narrow, shady, crooked alleys of the Arab section that fascinated us most. It is impossible for tourists like us to absorb that teeming, confusing spectacle: the merchants in their cave-like stalls hawking their wares; ragged children darting under foot; old porters bent under loads of baskets and crates; beggars of all ages and deformities; women with massive weights on their heads, their chests and bellies thrust forward like moving caryatids.

The much acclaimed new Israeli museum in Jerusalem disappointed me. The climb from the taxi-stop at the ticket window to the exhibition halls, in the cruel glare of sunlight in that bare, tree-less area seems endless. Noguchi's sculpture garden, with its still stronger glare due to the white pebbles in it which reflect the sunlight sharply, is impossible. (When my wife complained to Sir Philip Hendy, the newly appointed director of the museum, that there wasn't even a blade of grass in that garden, he replied, "It's not supposed to have any grass." "Then it's like a desert," exclaimed my wife. "I'm fond of deserts," Sir Philip said.)

With a few exceptions the sculpture there is atrocious.

I was irritated by the interior of the museum as well: by its low, heavy, oppressive ceilings and unsatisfactory lighting. Except for the rich collection of Judaica, its contents are meagre. One feels there is a wish to fill it with "names," so it has a Cézanne, a Gauguin, a Utrillo and a Kandinsky, none of them outstanding. The rest is what you see in any so-called modern museum anywhere: content-less pictures in the "international" style by artists with inflated reputations, plus all the claptrap of the moment.

The museum was holding a Chaim Soutine exhibition while we were there. Individually his intensely personal portraits, still-lifes and landscapes seem wonderful to me, but their collective impact was lost in the way they were presented. There seems to be something organically wrong with this museum. But on the same grounds is the Shrine of the Book, an appropriate structure of stone which houses ancient, excavated parchments relating to the history of the Jews. This smaller structure makes more sense functionally, historically and poetically.

Tel Aviv seems to be the cultural center in Israel, in a cosmopolitan sense, with its bookshops in various languages, its art museums and galleries. The Mann Auditorium is more pleasing than any glittering structure in Lincoln Center. There we met the seventy-five-year-old Reuben Rubin, painter, architect, sculptor and diplomat. I think of him as a kind of Rivera. Like Rivera he spent his early years studying and exhibiting in Europe, but returned at intervals to paint in his homeland of Palestine. He finally settled in Israel and, like Rivera, discarded the European influences. Like the Mexican's, his subject matter became steeped in the life and lore of the land and its people. He found a new style for this content, a kind of oriental neo-primitivism somewhat akin to Persian miniature, but on a mural scale.

In Rubin's Tel Aviv home hangs his painting of a feast, a sort of "Marriage at Cana," where, around a white-covered table with a still-life of food and drink, sit Arabs and Jews, with himself, his beautiful wife and young son among them. "I even invited Christ to this party," he said, pointing to a white-clad, bearded young Arab at one end of the table.

During that early period he painted the famous "Dancers at Meron" and a picture of pioneers against a background of sand and rocks, and extraordinary portraits of the philosopher Ahad Ha'am, of the playwright Peretz Hirschbein and his wife, and of himself with his family. Lately he has been painting landscapes of Israel's hills and olive groves, and rich, wild bouquets of flowers. As he says, "I paint what I love—my people, my family, my country. To paint means to sing."

Indeed there is in his work a singing, a lyrical quality.

None of Rubin's joyousness, of his inner peace, his confidence about his place in Israeli art, did I find in Naftali Bezem, the much younger Tel Aviv painter. In discussing his work he often uses the phrase "I despair." He told me that long ago he "gave up the effort of representing nature as it appears, because mankind, which means also me, has invented other means of doing it, so that artists can occupy themselves with other human experiences."

According to Bezem, he is influenced by pre-Renaissance art because "it did not concern itself with representing nature." (I disagree; Giotto, Duccio, Fra Angelico and Lorenzetti, among others, painted everything visible in this world.) In these conversations I found him searching but inconsistent, often enmeshed in sophistry and semantics. He considers himself a "figurative, un-realistic painter." He feels that realistic art is powerless to describe such events as the Nazi extermination of the Jews or the atomic destruction of Hiroshima. "I personally lean to a certain symbolism, which, together with the clear colors and bold outlines, will enable me to say something personal to some other people, and enrich their life."

I agreed with Bezem that it is impossible to paint the Nazi and Hiroshima horrors, or those of Vietnam, or the world turmoil of today, because other media perform this function. But I deplore this weakening of the role of the artist. For my part, I see no salvation in "a certain symbolism." Ultimately it leads to the extinction of the art known to us for thousands of years.

There is confusion in the mind of this talented artist, and I understand the reason for his occasional despair. For, after all his apologia, his work is a conglomeration of influences of the pallid masters of the twentieth century: the recent work of Picasso, the decorations of Léger, the much repeated symbols of Chagall, the doodles of Paul Klee.

The third Israeli artist we met was Anna Ticho, the outstanding draftsman. She is elderly and still lives in the rambling old Arab house in Jerusalem in which

Naftali Bezem

Anna Ticho

her late husband, the eminent eye surgeon, Dr. Abraham Ticho, received his patients for many years. The little street now bears his name.

Anna Ticho's work reflects a deep, lifelong familiarity with the landscape around Jerusalem, which she depicts in all seasons and at all hours of the day. She works exclusively in black and white, yet she creates an amazing illusion of color. At times her drawings tend toward surrealism and semi-abstraction, but even in these there is the reality of the Israeli landscape, the substance and texture of its rocks and earth.

June 6, 1968

Agnon's friend and neighbor who took us to visit him told us that the old man is not in very good health, that he may be distant, and even annoyed by us. "And no sketches," he said emphatically.

We found Agnon with a book, in his garden. Politely he invited us into the house. Some attempts were made at conversation in Yiddish or Hebrew, and after a while I said, "Mr. Agnon, before I came I took a drink or two. My tongue is untied and I feel bold enough to tell you that when I was very young, my father, who would be about a hundred years old if he were alive today, used to talk about a young and very talented Hebrew writer in Palestine by the name of Agnon. And now I'm privileged to meet this young writer who became a Nobel Prize winner."

Agnon looked at me through inflamed, teary eyes and asked in a quiet voice, "Who was your father?" When I answered "Avrohom Shoer," his face lit up and he rose and warmly shook my hand. Speaking softly as if to himself, he murmured, "Avrohom Shoer. I read his stories. He wrote in Hadoar. He was a writer and teacher."

Then Agnon brought out wine and cookies and called his wife, a frail old lady with a biblical face, and said to her, "This man's father was a Hebrew writer and storyteller."

Now our conversation was relaxed and warm. Agnon even consented to my drawing him, and I made a quick sketch of him and his wife while we were talking. In answer to my rather careless question as to who his favorite writers were, he said, "Well, one's favorites change as one grows older. There is Tolstoy . . . people mention him . . . I read your Dreiser, but what I remember is his unfavorable allusion to Jews in one of his autobiographical works . . . *Babbitt*— what was the name of the author? The book I never tire of reading is the Bible. This is the only thing I now read because of my bad eyes. Tomorrow I'm seeing the doctor about them."

At this point someone mentioned the unbelievable news that Robert Kennedy had been shot. We talked about violence in our country—where was it leading to?—about the unfortunate Kennedy family. Agnon said quietly as if to himself, "*Haim hatoo*" (they sinned), adding "Praised be the Lord that the attacker was not a Jew."

Both Agnon and his wife walked with us through the garden. He picked some fresh stems from a low bush, handed them to my delighted wife and said,

Woman and Plant

Reuben Rubin

I. Y. Agnon and His Wife

"Rosemary." Mrs. Agnon then picked another twig and gave it to her, saying, "Daphne." Her large sunken eyes were warm and smiling.

"It was your father Avrohom, after all, who introduced you to Agnon," Rebecca said to me as we walked to the car.

Vienna—June 11, 1968

I'm beginning to think that I'm a frustrated Expressionist, for I am so often drawn to the work of Georg Grosz, Otto Dix and Egon Schiele. I shall be haunted for a long time by the spastically gesturing figures and contorted faces of Egon Schiele's drawings, shown at the Albertina in Vienna in commemoration of the fiftieth anniversary of his death. He died at the age of twenty-eight during the 1918 influenza epidemic. Only at the end of his short life was he able to master oil painting, but from the very beginning he was a great draftsman.

It is hard to understand such early mastery of drawing; it usually takes a lifetime to achieve. As Tintoretto said so poetically, "Beautiful colors are for sale in the shops of the Rialto, but good drawing can only be fetched from the casket of the artist's talent with patient study and sleepless nights."

Paris—June 14, 1968

Like a chain-letter, we have been referred to people from New York to Budapest to Prague to Dresden to East Berlin. Everyone has gone out of his way to welcome us and show us what his country has been able to accomplish in spite of difficulties created by the hostility between East and West.

In Prague we came upon a small but choice collection of nineteenth- and twentieth-century paintings. There were two Daumiers: his best "Laundress," a heroic figure of a woman hurrying with her child, their shadows merging on the ground; and "The Family at the Barricades," unusually colorful. There were also Courbets, Corots, Pissarros, Cézannes, and a silly but wonderful full-length self-portrait by that inimitable primitive, Henri Rousseau, holding a palette inscribed "Josephine," and standing against a background of bridges, ships, flags and flying balloons.

I stood for a long time in front of Delacroix's study for his masterpiece "Massacre at Scio"—that of the wounded and dying woman with a child clinging to her breast. This study recalled to my mind my conversations with the Israeli artist, Naftali Bezem. I agreed with him then that today artists could not adequately depict the massive horrors of our civilization. This live child, however, clinging to a dying mother, makes me retract what I said then. In such a detail it is possible to express a Vietnam or an Auschwitz. All the modern media of communication notwithstanding, one would wish to conjure up a Daumier, a Delacroix.

Berlin—July 1, 1968

If it were not for the collection of old masters in Dahlem, I would not bother coming to West Berlin. This is the third time I've been here, and my impression of this sector remains unchanged. The part of West Berlin that was not damaged is dull, gray and ordinary, and to me the new structures are architecturally distasteful, modernistically angular, awkwardly spaced and clashing with one another in their proportions.

East Berlin seems more beautiful, especially now that many of its graceful old buildings have been restored to their original state. Even the new buildings with their uniformly cold façades do not protrude too much as yet. There are still many empty spaces, some of which have been utilized to form well-proportioned squares paved with small cobblestones. I felt that West Berlin was busy, thriving, pursuing wealth, while East Berlin was quiet and austere, with a busy cultural life.

In East Berlin we met two sculptors: Fritz Cremer, who designed the Buchenwald Memorial and whose work we saw in the National Gallery (I especially liked his self-portrait as a dying soldier); and Rene Graetz, a charming, sophisticated, restless character, a self-styled admirer of Henry Moore who told me that his "sculpture is realistic" but his "graphic work is not." We had a lively discussion about art. I talked about the many paintings I've seen in European museums, how I store them in my head and how I like to compare them in my mind with one another, unhistorically, without system or theory. I used Malraux's phrase "museums without walls," referring to the paintings in my head.

This aroused unanimous disagreement. I was told it was "useless" and "not correct" to do so, and the mention of Malraux brought forth a critical outburst from the hitherto silent Fritz Cremer: "Malraux's theory that art has not made any progress is sheer nonsense!" He went on to say that art is making progress, along with social progress and with the discovery of new materials. Unoriented as I am to this historical approach to art, I heard myself declaring,

"Art does *not* progress" with which, to my surprise, the unpredictable Rene Graetz suddenly agreed. I said no more, and incorrigibly I mentally compared Otto Dix's World War I "Triptych," which I had just seen in Dresden, with Goya's execution paintings and with Picasso's "Guernica."

To my great pleasure, in East Berlin we met again Gabriele Mucchi, the Italian painter, about whom I wrote in *Homage to Thomas Eakins, Etc.* We renewed our acquaintance, and he said to me in German: "Raphael Soyer, as socialists and painters, let us address each other as 'Du'" (the familiar form of *you*). I was delighted and honored by the remark.

Paris—July 17, 1968

Today we had guests. Since we have a small apartment in a Montparnasse hotel, for the first time in Europe we were able to be hosts. Two of our daughter Mary's friends, former classmates, came with their families; the room was alive with active children. We were charmed by them and were seized with longing to see our own little grandsons, David and Joey, and their mother and father. We were homesick for New York, and suddenly we felt that our vacation had been prolonged to the point of near-boredom. Though I filled my sketchbook, I still had too much time to spare. There were mornings when I'd wake up and mutter to myself, "What the dickens am I doing here?"

I've come to the end. I've written myself out.

I think I'm one of the few who paint directly from nature today. My palette is a wooden rectangle. There is a self-portrait of Rembrandt in the outskirts of London in which he holds a palette like mine. When Edward Hopper once showed me the over-sized easel he had made himself, I exclaimed, "Why, it's like the easel used by St. Luke painting the Madonna and Child in medieval Flemish pictures!"

How primitive are the tools with which I paint! How ancient is the art of painting as I know it! Can it still be the art for our times? Such thoughts are always with me while I work, for better or for worse.

How autobiographical my art is. All these portraits of myself, my parents the members of my family; the pictures of the artists with whom I came in contact; the city I have known, and its people; the few landscapes of Maine— I have revealed myself in them long before this rambling chronicle was conceived, not only by the usual automatic revelation of the artist's personality, but through the subject matter which is my life.

About the Author

Born on December 25, 1899, in Russia, Raphael Soyer came to this country with his family in 1912, and in the following years studied drawing and painting at Cooper Union, the National Academy of Design, and with Guy Pène Du Bois at the Art Students League.

Mr. Soyer's first one-man show was at the Daniel Gallery in 1929. Other shows were held at the Valentine Gallery, Associated American Artists, the Babcock, Rehn, and, most recently, the Forum Gallery.

In 1967 the Whitney Museum gave a retrospective exhibition of Mr. Soyer's work. He has taught at the Art Students League, The New School, and the National Academy of Design, and is a member of the American Institute of Arts and Letters and the National Academy. He is the author of two previous books, *Painter's Pilgrimage* and *Homage to Thomas Eakins, Etc.*

Books About Raphael Soyer

Raphael Soyer, monograph No. 19, American Artists Group
Raphael Soyer: Paintings and Drawings by Walter K. Gutman, Shorewood Press, 1960
Raphael Soyer by Lloyd Goodrich, The Whitney Museum, 1967
Raphael Soyer: Fifty Years of Print Making, compiled by Sylvan Cole, Jr. with a foreword
    by Jacob Kainen, Da Capo Press, 1967
Raphael Soyer: Drawings and Watercolors by Joseph K. Foster, Crown Publishers, 1968

The text of SELF-REVEALMENT was composed in English Monotype Bembo and printed with the monochrome illustrations by Clarke & Way, Inc., New York. The color illustrations were printed by Offset und Buchdruck, Zurich, Switzerland. The color photographs were made by Robert Gruen. The binding was done by A. Horowitz and Son, Clifton, New Jersey. Format by the Bert Clarke Design Group.